Gregg Popovich: The Inspiring Life and Leadership Lessons of One of Basketball's Greatest Coaches

An Unauthorized Biography & Leadership Case Study

Table of Contents

Foreword

Often regarded as one of, if not the greatest coach in the NBA, Gregg Popovich demands the respect and admiration of both players and coaches around the league. This is with good reason, as he has been a driving factor for the San Antonio Spurs' decades of success and perennial playoff contention. What makes Pop so impressive has been how he has adapted the style of his team's play to the trends of the league over time and how he has gotten superstar-caliber players to commit to his system of success while often sacrificing personal statistics or recognition. Thank you for purchasing *Gregg Popovich: The Inspiring Life and Leadership Lessons of One of Basketball's Greatest Coaches.* In this unauthorized biography and leadership case study, we will learn some of the background behind Gregg Popovich's incredible life story, and more importantly his impact on the game of basketball. In the last section of the book, we'll learn what makes Gregg Popovich such an effective leader and coach, including a review of key takeaways that you can remember when looking to apply lessons from Gregg Popovich to your own life. Hope you enjoy and if you do, please do not forget to leave a review!

Also, check out my website at claytongeoffreys.com to join my exclusive list where I let you know about my latest books. To thank you for your purchase, you can go to my site to download a free copy of *33 Life Lessons: Success Principles, Career Advice & Habits of Successful People*. In the book, you'll learn from some of the greatest thought leaders of different industries on what it takes to become successful and how to live a great life.

Cheers,

Clayton Geoffreys

Visit me at www.claytongeoffreys.com

Introduction

Much like how soldiers are the reasons why countries win battles, players are the reasons why NBA teams win games on the hardwood floor. The countless hours they put into honing and crafting their game in the gym and weight room contributes to how they affect the outcome of games. They sacrifice and pour out their sweat, tears, and even blood for the purpose of giving wins to their teams and fans.

But while NBA games are won by the players on the floor, preparation and strategy have always been the keys to winning championships. Soldiers may be the reasons why battles are won, but wars are won outside of the battlefield. And in the NBA, players may be the reasons why teams win games, but championships are won by the leadership of their coaches. And when it comes down to coaching, one would be hard-pressed to find someone better than Gregg Popovich in that department.

There have been many great coaches who have become legendary names in the history of the NBA. There was Red Auerbach, who was a revolutionary at making his team focus on making each other better on his way to nine NBA championships during the 1960s era of the league. While relying on Bill Russell's leadership on the floor, the Boston Celtics were winning titles and dominating because of how Auerbach instilled in them the basics and fundamentals of team play.

Decades later, Pat Riley made the Los Angeles Lakers the best NBA show on the planet by running a fast-paced system that relied on the fast break and the passing skills of the legendary Magic Johnson. Riley won four titles with the Lakers back in the 1980s and would later win one again with the Miami Heat in 2006 at the tail end of his coaching career.

Then came Phil Jackson. Jackson relied on the Triangle Offense system to harness the skills of

Michael Jordan, who is widely regarded as the best player to have ever set foot on a basketball court, and of Scottie Pippen. Jackson's "Zen" beliefs also helped him get his team mentally and spiritually prepared for every game while leading the Chicago Bulls to six NBA titles in the 1990s. He then instilled the same system and beliefs in the Los Angeles Lakers in the 2000s to guide them to five NBA championships under the on-court leadership of Shaquille O'Neal and Kobe Bryant.

And then there is Gregg Popovich. Yes, there have been coaches who have won more or the same number of NBA titles that Gregg Popovich has won. But the man that has led the San Antonio Spurs on the strategic end of the floor was always one of the more, if not the most, consistent head coaches the league has seen in recent history.

Gregg Popovich, or "Pop" as he is often called, has a *résumé* that stands out among all the other active coaches in the league today. He has won five titles since he started coaching the Spurs back in 1996. In his 20 years of experience with the team, he has always made the San Antonio Spurs consistent contenders in the league despite core players coming and going.

Pop won his first title at the tail end of David Robinson's career when Tim Duncan was still an inexperienced youngster. He then won more championships when Duncan was in his prime as a lone star in San Antonio. And even when his core star players were in the waning years of their NBA careers, Pop was able to still win a title in 2014 against the Miami Heat, who had three superstars in their prime.

And even when Gregg Popovich was not winning titles with the Spurs, he was always the reason why San Antonio was a force in the NBA for two decades. From 1997 up to 2017, the San Antonio Spurs' winning percentage never dropped under 60. That is an amazing accomplishment. And while his team won 37 in a shortened, 50-game season back in 1999, it was the equivalent of 61 wins in a regular 82-game season. In those 20 years, Pop has won 60 or more games six times and always made the playoffs with the San Antonio Spurs until 2019, even though the Spurs' winning percentage saw a drop off from 2017.

What was most impressive about how Gregg Popovich was making the Spurs consistent title contenders every single year was how he was doing it when his core players were coming, going, and aging. He did have a core Big Three composed of Tim Duncan, Tony Parker, and Manu Ginóbili for the most part, but he proved that he was able to win games even when his best players were on their decline. The Spurs remained as consistent as ever as Pop was making his team play the right way and developing overlooked players into contributors and role players. He relied on his Big Three to bail the team out in tough situations but, in most cases, the San Antonio Spurs were always about great team play that allowed even the last guy on the bench to contribute.

Outside of 1997's top overall pick Tim Duncan, Pop has always had a knack for getting the best out of players that nobody thought would make it to the NBA. Tony Parker was drafted 28th back in 2001 but would turn out to become a multiple-time All-Star and a four-time NBA champion. Manu Ginóbili was selected second to last in 1999 but would go on to win more titles than any of the top-10 draft picks of that year. Meanwhile, Kawhi Leonard was selected outside the top 10 in his draft year and was merely seen as a possible three-and-D player in the NBA, but has since become the best two-way player the league has seen recently.

Popovich's role players have often been overlooked by others—yet never by him. He strategically harnessed the specialties of niche players like Bruce Bowen, Rasho Nesterovic, Brent Barry, Danny Green, Boris

Diaw, and Matt Bonner, among others, to perfectly match the skills of his core players. He was able to do that for more than three decades and has made a career of turning G-League players into legitimate and valuable contributors in the NBA.

Aside from developing role players, Pop has always had a talent for finding gems outside the United States. In addition to the French player, Tony Parker, and the Argentinian Manu Ginóbili, he has also tapped the services of foreign players such as Rasho Nesterovic, Boris Diaw, Tiago Splitter, Cory Joseph, and more. He has made the Spurs a gateway for international players to get to the NBA and make a name for themselves. At one point, his team was even predominantly comprised of foreign players who were overlooked and unwanted before they made their way to the San Antonio Spurs.

But making his team play basketball "the right way" was Gregg Popovich's calling card for success. Back when the league was celebrating the athleticism and highlight-reel plays of superstars in the 2000s, Pop had his team play a slow-paced, defensive style that suffocated opposing teams. A decade later, he made the Spurs a model of team play. The ball moved around so much that it was easy to find open looks for anyone. He had his team shooting three-pointers in bunches while never letting them forget to look for the best available shot. They were passing the ball so much that it became difficult for defenses to adjust and read the offense. It was a Spurs team oozing with chemistry and every play on the floor looked magical.

With that in mind, Gregg Popovich's leadership skills were never in question. He may look and act like a strict disciplinarian and a man of few words, especially during on-court interviews, but everyone around and under him loves what he brings to the team and organization. Pop has always been a model of consistency. He knows how to look for players with the right skills and attitude. He surrounds himself with staff that have the same potential to grow and develop.

In fact, many of his assistants have gone on to become successful coaches themselves. This includes Steve Kerr, Mike Budenholzer, Avery Johnson, and Quin Snyder.

Given all that, perhaps the best way to describe Pop is by calling him the model leader, a visionary who never ceases to make everyone around him better by helping them reach their potential.

Chapter 1: Background Story

Early Life

Gregg Popovich was born on January 28, 1949. Though the soon-to-be-legendary head coach was born in East Chicago, Indiana, he barely had any American blood in him. His father Raymond was of Serbian descent, while his mother, Katherine, was from Croatia. Despite his international background, Pop would be every bit as American as one could get.

Popovich started playing basketball early in his life and was one of the best young players in the country. When he was a young boy, he was part of the 1960 Gary Biddy All-Star Team. "Biddy Basketball" was much the same as the regular game but had slight differences. The height of the basket was only about eight-and-a-half feet compared to the standard 10-foot basket used in the standard regular game. There was also a player height limit of 5'6" in Biddy Basketball. This catered to shorter and smaller young players like the 11-year-old Pop. His team would win third place in the World Tournament held that same year.[i]

Gregg Popovich would later attend Merrillville High School. Back then, Pop was known as "Popo," his first truc nickname, by his teammates. The man now known for his strands of neat white hair used to sport a slick brown 'do in those days. Despite not being the tallest player on the team, the young guard had long legs that jived with his aggressive style of play. Gregg Popovich, the patient, wise coach we know now was quite different in his youth. He was an impatient boy that could not wait for his turn. He wanted to be the best and was in a hurry to get to that point.[ii]

In 1966, he went on to study at the United States Air Force Academy. That was when things started to really take a turn for the better for Gregg. The kid that could not wait his turn back in Merrillville learned how to become a more disciplined young man. His style and attitude in high school did not mesh with how they did things at the Air Force Academy. Things started to change for Pop as he eventually grew to become a more disciplined person who remained calm, poised, and patient at all times.

His former teammate at the Academy, Dave Kapaska, once called the Air Force Academy a leadership training laboratory. They not only molded young men who were willing to serve the country but developed future leaders as well. Then again, Kapaska also said that the younger recruits were first taught how to become servants and followers. Gregg Popovich had to become a follower first.[ii]

The challenge for Pop back then was not how to become a leader. Leadership was never too difficult for Gregg Popovich. He was a natural at that. One could even say he was born with that quality. However, he was never the best follower. He was the type of young man who did not want to follow behind people he knew were not as good as he was.[ii] That was one of the rials he had to undertake on his way to the ideal leader he is today.

A former assistant coach at the Air Force Academy, Hank Egan, once said that Gregg could not reconcile being a leader and a follower at the same time. When things did not go his way, he would sometimes show an attitude that was likened to that of a spoiled child. Egan coached Pop in his first two years with the Academy.[ii] He knew and saw how much of a struggle it was to coach the headstrong young man.

One memory that never left Egan's mind was how Popovich always made it known to him every single day that he did not belong on the junior varsity team. Pop could not wait. He believed that he should be playing for the varsity team back then when others thought he had to wait for his turn and learn to be a follower instead of a leader right away. While Popovich believed it was a mistake to leave him off varsity, he would soon learn enough patience to work his way onto the team the right way, without trying to force himself into something he was not actually ready for yet.[ii]

Even for a guard, Gregg was a pretty good post player in his days with the Academy. But for his size, he was better off playing facing the basket and handling the ball. He worked on those aspects of the game maniacally. For a busy cadet that had little free time, Pop would go to the gym nearly every night to practice on his fundamentals. He dribbled with the lights turned off to improve his handles. He also used unorthodox methods to improve his balance.[ii]

Bert Spear, his teammate and the varsity coach's son, commented that he was even hungrier during practices. He played defense like it was a real game. The brave Gregg Popovich of today had already manifested at an early age. Much like how he treats his stars and his role players alike, he treated his teammates equally as well and was never afraid to get in their faces whenever he saw something wrong. He never backed down against bigger and stronger guys regardless of whether they were the best players or the last guys on the bench.[ii]

By the time Gregg had proven himself worthy, newer and younger teammates looked up to him with delight. It was often an Air Force Academy practice to bully freshman cadets. However, Pop was different. He always treated people equally no matter how good or bad, or how young or old they were. Pop was more interested in making new friends among the freshmen.[ii]

It was also during his Air Force Academy days when Gregg formed a bond that would ultimately be for the longest of terms. Pop had enjoyed spending time with team trainer Jim Conboy, whom he would later room with when he became an assistant with the team. His friendship with Conboy led to him meeting the trainer's daughter Erin, whom he would later marry.[ii]

It was in 1970 when Gregg finished his studies with the Air Force Academy. He graduated with a degree in Soviet Studies, which he frequently used when he toured around Eastern Europe as a member of the U.S. Air Force Basketball Team. Aside from being one of the better players on the floor, he used his studies of the Russian language to get his coaches in touch with the other team's strategies.[ii]

When Pop returned to the United States in 1972, Olympic tryouts for the basketball team were scheduled to be held at the Air Force Academy. Luckily, Pop had connections. Jack Herron Jr., the son of one of the assistants and recruiters for the Academy back when Popovich was still with the team, was a member of the selection committee for the Olympic team. He knew how good Pop was, especially when he was playing extremely well overseas. He wanted Popovich to get an invite to the team.[ii]

Tryouts were divided into teams of 10 to 12 members, considering the large selection pool that the committee had to work with. Popovich was assigned to Indiana coaching legend Bobby Knight, who believed that only two players in his pool had a chance of making the team. Because of that, Knight had all the players pass the ball to those two guys.[ii]

One of those two players was a forward named Bobby Jones. Jones recalls his stint with Popovich. When all the other players on the team were jacking up shots and trying to impress the selection committee, Gregg was out there on the floor playing the way he was used to. He took the shots he knew he could take while making the right plays. He made the right passes without being flashy and ended up leading the team in shooting percentage because of how well he knew his spots. His style of play back then mirrored the way he coaches his teams today. His teams and players were never flashy and never took bad shots. They made the right passes to open teammates to convert on the best possible shots available.

Despite his lack of flash, Gregg was in serious contention for an Olympic spot. However, Herron remembers how biased members of the selection committee were. Coaches of various players selected in the pool suddenly sprouted out of nowhere to vote for their guys. It was politically motivated, as then-Celtics coach Tommy Heinsohn would say. Heinsohn believed that Popovich belonged on that team but knew he was not going to be selected because of the politics involved.[ii]

Despite his calm demeanor, Gregg was immensely disappointed and frustrated that he was not chosen to play for the Olympic team. After all, he relied solely on his merits without asking any coach or committee member to champion his cause. Moreover, he thought that the team was more flashy and offensive-minded than fundamentally-sound. Pop thought that the

Olympic team lacked defense—a part of the floor he takes a lot of pride in.

Fast-forward to 2012 and we have proof of how much Gregg Popovich emphasizes the importance of defense when he asked for Bruce Bowen's number to be retired. Bowen was a specialist on only one side of the floor— he was the best perimeter defender in the league during his prime, but his offense was severely lacking. Despite that, Pop showed how much he valued Bowen's defensive contributions by getting his number retired.

Fast-forward again to 2016 and lo and behold, we find Gregg Popovich coaching the Olympic team in the backdraft of a highly successful and illustrious career. Fate sometimes works in mysterious ways, and clearly, it has worked in Pop's favor.

Early Coaching Years

Gregg Popovich would serve his required active duty with the United States Air Force while also taking an active role with the force's basketball team during those years. After his service, he stayed true to his roots with the Air Force by coming back to the Academy in 1973 to work as an assistant coach to Hank Egan, who was the head coach at that time.

Pop did have aspirations of playing NBA ball and even tried out, albeit unsuccessfully, for the Denver Nuggets in 1975, but coaching seemed to always be his true calling. And Pop was never stagnant during his early coaching years. The young assistant coach attended the University of Denver during those years to earn his master's degree in Physical Education.

By the time he had earned his master's degree, and after serving as an assistant with the Air Force Academy, Popovich accepted his first head coaching job in 1979. He would go on to become the head coach of the Pomona-Pitzer Sagehens, a team composed of two separate colleges that played in Division III of the NCAA. For the first time in 68 years, Pomona-Pitzer won a title when Popovich led the team to a championship in 1986.

Despite winning a title, Pop's career with the Sagehens was not as smooth as one might think. In his first season coaching the team, Pomona-Pitzer ended the season 2-22. The following year, they improved to 10-15 but would spend the next four seasons as a mediocre squad before they surprisingly won the title in 1986, even though the team only finished with a record of 16-12.

After eight seasons with the Division III school, Popovich took a temporary sabbatical from the team, which was a customary school practice. During that time, Popovich never stopped trying to get better as a coach. He asked his former coach, Bert Spear, to give him a spot in North Carolina to learn under the legendary head coach Dean Smith, who had coached Michael Jordan to a title in college just a few seasons ago.

Pop would spend only three months with the champion coach in Chapel Hill, but he made the most out of his stay. He spent hundreds of hours watching Dean Smith's instructional videos. He barely ever missed observing the team's practices and often conversed with the Tar Heels' assistants. He described that experience as an excellent opportunity for him to get his thoughts more organized.[iii]

It was also during those three months under Dean Smith that Pop got to reconnect with a future Hall-of-Fame coach. Larry Brown visited the school campus where he had spent time as a basketball star back in the1960s. It was there where he once again met Gregg Popovich, who had impressed him back in 1972 during the Olympic tryouts.

After that brief stint with North Carolina, Popovich moved over to Kansas, another Division I school, to become a temporary part of head coach Larry Brown's staff. (Brown would later become one of the winningest head coaches in NBA history. In fact, Brown is the only coach in basketball history to win both an NCAA national championship and an NBA title.) Brown immediately saw talent in Pop, whom he thought was not as engaged as he wanted to be in North Carolina. The Kansas staff also included future NBA coaches Alvin Gentry and R. C. Buford.[ii]

R. C. Buford eventually became one of Pop's best friends and confidants. At the time, nobody expected the unlikely pair of Popovich and Buford to become friends. Gregg Popovich was an extrovert who liked to have fun with his fellow staff members and players. He was a simple man that took the bus to work every day. On the other hand, Buford was a quiet introvert who was probably wealthier than the rest of Kansas' coaching staff combined. However, both Pop and R. C. had the same philosophy when it came to basketball coaching ideas. It was through their similar beliefs that Popovich and Buford connected with one another.

Meanwhile, Larry Brown loved what he had with those two great minds as part of his support system and would often promote discussion between them so that they could learn from one another, just as much as Brown was able to learn from his two assistant coaches.[ii]

Pop also forged a close and lasting connection with Brown that year, a bond that would stretch well into the future. Brown once said about Pop, "With that year we spent [at Kansas], we just became best friends." But just how close did Pop and Larry Brown really become? Suffice it to say, Pop and Brown would be seeing a whole lot of each other professionally, along with Buford, in the very near future. And from the personal side of things? Well, Pop was the best man at Brown's wedding.

Gregg Popovich's time spent with North Carolina and Kansas marked a real turning point in his development as a coach and would prove to be instrumental in his quest for a successful career in the NBA. Though Pop returned to Pomona-Pitzer to coach one final season for the Sagehens in 1987-88, greater things were on the horizon.

Chapter 2: NBA Coaching Career

The Move to San Antonio

In 1988, Larry Brown accepted the head coaching job for a San Antonio Spurs team that was never very successful following the merger of the NBA and ABA back in the middle of the 1970s. While they had George Gervin from the late 70s up to the early 80s, the team never won titles and were regularly in the middle of the pack or worse when it came to how competitive the franchise was. Things were looking pretty bleak by the mid-80s—until Brown took the job.

Brown immediately invited Gregg Popovich and R. C. Buford over to San Antonio to join his staff. Of course, the two bright minds accepted the offer and moved to Texas to become legitimate NBA coaches, albeit assistants to Larry Brown. But even after becoming part of an NBA franchise and earning more money than he had ever earned before, Popovich stayed true to his simple roots and to himself.

Larry Brown once described Pop's apartment at that time as a "three-furniture space." He had a bed, a sofa, and a chair.[ii] That was it. Just like the Spurs of today's era, Gregg Popovich was never flashy. He was more focused on learning the ins and outs of the game and trying to improve himself as a strategist than on wasting time on trivial matters and material objects that never really mattered in the grandest scheme of things. In a sense, Gregg Popovich thought the only things that mattered were thoughts and ideas—particularly those that he believed made the team better. Even Larry Brown himself was not spared from Pop's constant discussions about his new schemes and ideas for the team.

However, things did not start all that smoothly for Gregg Popovich's career as an NBA assistant coach. The San Antonio Spurs had a long way to go and a lot of work to do. They were dreadfully horrible during the 1988-89 NBA season, so much so that they ended the season 21-61—dead last in their division. However, this was only a hiccup on the cusp of the team's metamorphosis, for vast improvements were already in the works. David Robinson, who was drafted in 1987 but had to serve in the Navy first, had finally joined the Spurs. A season later, Robinson's presence on a team coached by bright minds helped the San Antonio Spurs win 56 games to complete what was then the best single-season turnaround in league history.

With a legitimate NBA superstar manning the paint for the San Antonio Spurs, life got easier for the coaching staff. But Brown, leading a small-market team such as the Spurs, had to make cuts to save money. He hated cutting and waiving players and gave the task to none other than his stern yet honest assistant, Gregg Popovich.[ii]

During his third season with the Spurs in 1991, Gregg Popovich was given the unenviable task of telling point guard Avery Johnson that he was being waived from the team. That was one of the most memorable and oddly feel-good moments for a guard technically fired from his job. Johnson remembered how Pop told him straight-faced that he had been cut from the Spurs. Popovich then said that he was good enough to belong to the league and that some other team would surely take him after he was cleared off the waivers.[ii] Pop was always that kind of a man. He was always stern and strict but could appreciate hard work whenever he saw it.

In the middle of the 1991-92 season, Larry Brown, known for his nomadic ways, suddenly left the team. The organization's owner said that Brown himself asked to be fired after a rough start to the season.

Buford thought that Pop would get the nod as Brown's replacement. However, general manager Bob Bass took over the job as the interim head coach.

The following season, Bob Bass hired Jerry Tarkanian to become the new head coach of the team instead of either Gregg Popovich or R. C. Buford. Neither of the two even had a place on the team, though Pop would claim that he was offered a minor role in the film room, a job that was beneath his credentials and expertise at that time. It would not be long, however, before Bass discovered what a mistake it was to hire Tarkanian instead of Pop. The former UNLV head coach would not even last half a season before he was let go. By that time, it was too late to give Pop the job.

A Short Stint with the Golden State Warriors

Don Nelson, who would soon go on to become the winningest head coach in NBA history, hired Gregg Popovich as his assistant for the Golden State Warriors. However, his primary function with the team was to act as an intermediary between star players Chris Webber and Don Nelson, who were both cold to one another and seemed to be suffering from "irreconcilable differences" with the way they approached the game of basketball. Unlike Nelson, Pop had the guts to tell Webber and Nelson what they needed to know. He was always a disciplinarian that treated players equally, no matter how good or bad they were. You could always count on Pop to tell it like it was.

It was also at Golden State when Gregg Popovich reunited with the point guard that was cut from San Antonio a few seasons before. Pop was the one behind bringing Avery Johnson to the Warriors, as he knew how hard the scrappy little point guard worked to get better. While other coaches only looked at stats and size, Pop also looked at a player's attitude, work ethic, and basketball IQ. He liked what he saw in Johnson, despite the fact that he was only 5'10" and was never a standout player in any of the NBA teams he had played for in the past.

Return to the Spurs, Becoming the Head Coach

In 1994, Peter Holt purchased the San Antonio Spurs franchise and would ultimately transform it into the model organization that it is today. One of the first and best moves that he made was to hire Gregg Popovich as the general manager and vice president of basketball operations. Since then, the landscape of not just Spurs basketball was changed, but also the entire NBA, as Gregg Popovich had complete control over all the basketball-related decisions on the Spurs franchise.

In a surprising move, Pop signed Avery Johnson (who had just been waived by Golden State) to become the team's lead guard, even after the little man was cut from the Spurs several seasons before. Pop continued to believe in Johnson, and his instinct would prove to be spot on, as Avery Johnson would go on to become a key player for the Spurs as well as a successful NBA coach himself in the future.

Popovich was also responsible for trading away defensive specialist and arguably the best rebounder in league history, Dennis Rodman, to the Chicago Bulls. Pop was not very fond of him. As good as Rodman was, Pop valued attitude above anything else. Dennis Rodman's personality was a little too unorthodox for his tastes.

At the start of the 1996-97 season, the San Antonio Spurs were only 3-15 through their first 18 games under head coach Bob Hill and had lost David Robinson to a season-ending injury. Pop made the decision to fire Hill, whom he had been dissatisfied with since the previous year when the Spurs failed to reach the Western Conference finals after being eliminated in the second round of the playoffs by the Utah Jazz. Then, in an even bolder move, he named himself the head coach of the team instead. Mind you, nobody expects an executive to demote himself to head coach. Pop did it because it was his passion and he believed it was the right thing for the team, but it still came as quite a shock.

At first, many people questioned Pop's decision to let head coach Bob Hill go. Hill had led the Spurs to a 62-win season a year ago with David Robinson playing like the MVP that he was. Moreover, Hill was a crowd favorite that had proven himself worthy as a legitimate NBA coach. However, in Popovich's eyes, Hill had been failing to correctly steer the ship following David Robinson's season-ending injury and he was not willing to let it continue.

Suddenly, it was Gregg Popovich who boarded the team bus as the head coach, telling his boys that he would be the new coach of the San Antonio Spurs. But the man had no previous head coaching experience outside of the Division III Pomona-Pitzer squad back in the 80s. He may have worked as an assistant with

Larry Brown and Don Nelson, but he was still a greenhorn in the NBA as a head coach. The Spurs fans even greeted him with jeers and disdain when the team came back home to play their first game in San Antonio following Bob Hill's departure. It was an ironic moment, for Gregg Popovich would hold that head coach position for a very long time. And decades later, the same exact fans will probably cry the day their beloved Pop finally decides to hang his boots up as a head coach.

Will Perdue, who was one of the Spurs' centers at that time, remembered how it happened. It was a road game, and Pop joined the team as an executive. One day, he suddenly came onto the bus and announced that he was replacing Bob Hill, who never came out to join the team. At first, Purdue thought Pop was joking, but then he realized it was true when the bus started moving without his former head coach.[iv]

Perdue's wife had an "I told you so" moment after the center relayed to her what had happened. She had long noticed how Gregg Popovich was seemingly unhappy as a general manager just watching from the sidelines. It was evident on Pop's face that he was not content being the man gathering the pieces of the puzzle to let another guy assemble them himself. Pop was the type of person that wanted to collect the pieces and assemble the entire puzzle by himself.[iv]

In his first year of what would become a legendary head coaching career, Pop struggled to win games because of the injuries that his key players suffered. San Antonio won only 20 games that season but ended up getting the top overall pick in the 1997 NBA Draft. That pick turned out to be Tim Duncan, who would start a long-lasting marriage of success with Gregg Popovich as arguably the greatest power forward in the history of the NBA.

Of course, nobody expected that team to win a lot that season. The team had revolved around David Robinson so much on both ends of the floor that it eventually collapsed without "The Admiral" manning the middle on offense and defense. The Spurs' weakness was exposed that season. They had a lot of good players that would look like stars on their best nights, but the system was focused too much on Robinson. Pop did not like that but had to work with the personnel that he had left in a season when injuries continued to plague the team like the common cold. Still, there was a valuable lesson to be learned that season—it was clear that he needed to veer away from hinging the team's success on a single player.

Chapter 3: Building the Spurs Dynasty

The Twin Towers Era

The road that Gregg Popovich took to get to the top coaching spot in the San Antonio Spurs organization was not an easy one. He had to start with a Division III school before getting noticed by Larry Brown late in the 80s. Yet even after showing his worth and strategic intelligence as an assistant, Spurs ownership still did not trust him. Opportunity did not come his way until after Peter Holt took over as the new owner and Pop helped revitalize the team.

However, the start of Gregg Popovich's journey to legendary status was still on its maiden voyage when he took over as head coach of the Spurs in 1996. The wheels began turning when the team drafted Tim Duncan out of Wake Forest in 1997. Duncan would spend the entirety of his career in San Antonio, much like how Pop did as a head coach.

Tim Duncan would go on to become a 15-time All-Star, a two-time MVP, and a five-time champion. And throughout all his accomplishments, Duncan remained level-headed and calm. He worked harder than anyone in the organization while staying faithful to the mantra that the team was above him. Furthermore, when Duncan was aging, he knew that his time as the team's alpha male was coming to an end. He did not mind giving the reigns to Tony Parker and the younger guys when the time came. He placed his ego out of the way while making sure he did what he was asked to do. In essence, he fit in perfectly with Gregg Popovich's system. Pop's influence and mentorship in Tim Duncan's career was evident, as he displayed the same qualities and work ethic that Pop himself evinced and valued. That was exactly the kind of player that Gregg Popovich wanted on his team.

With Tim Duncan and David Robinson in the middle, Pop suddenly shifted the team's focus from offense to defense. Bob Hill was a spectacular offensive coach when he was the man leading the Spurs. He had Robinson putting up monstrous MVP numbers. But all that changed when Gregg Popovich took over as head coach.

Pop continuously preached the value of defense and accountability, even when he was still in the early stages of his coaching career. He forced the team to shift its focus to defense. His guards played a huge role, though much of the credit would go to Duncan and Robinson—the "two towers"—inside the paint. Pop's defensive system focused on making his defenders hound the opposing team's ball-handler and to funnel the ball towards the big men in the paint. He had the team running plays and sequences all day long during practices to make sure that they would never falter on defense no matter who was on the floor.[iv]

As R. C. Buford himself would say, Gregg Popovich's defensive style did not only maximize what Robinson and Duncan could do on the floor as great defenders themselves but it also maximized what the entire roster could contribute on the defensive end. Buford said that Pop's decisions were focused on helping the entire team reach its defensive potential instead of just relying and maximizing on what great players could do at that end.[iv] Even though Robinson was a former Defensive Player of the Year and one of the best shot-blockers in league history, while Tim Duncan developed into one of the most consistent and reliable defensive big men in the NBA, Popovich never made it a point to focus only on what his big men could do as defenders but also maximized whatever capabilities his other players could do on the defensive end of the floor.

On the offensive end, Gregg Popovich simplified the way basketball was being played. He did not have a lot of offensive sets in a slow-paced system. Instead, he had his team practice on a few plays and made them run them countless times until they remembered those plays to the bone. It was a case of practicing ten moves a thousand times instead of practicing a thousand moves only ten times.

It would not take long for the Spurs to cash in on Tim Duncan's prowess and a much-improved San Antonio Spurs system under Pop's leadership. Timmy would immediately dominate the league alongside David Robinson to form a dreaded twin-tower combination, even though the latter had slowed down a bit with age and injuries. A year after averaging more than 21 points and nearly 12 rebounds in his rookie season, Duncan led the Spurs to the 1999 NBA Championship when the league was still recovering from Michael Jordan's second retirement.

In that season, the San Antonio Spurs won 37 of the 50 games they played in a shortened season. Knowing he had the size advantage against any other team in the league, Gregg Popovich employed a slow-paced defensive style that focused on getting the ball to one of his two big men in the paint when they were on the offense.

The strategy worked and the Spurs breezed through the first three rounds of the playoffs. Their only loss in the Western Conference playoff picture was in their first-round matchup against the Minnesota Timberwolves. They then easily swept the Los Angeles Lakers and Portland Trail Blazers in the next two rounds, though both teams had a lot of talent and depth. Then, in the Finals, they defeated the New York Knicks 4-1 to claim the franchise's first NBA title. Tim Duncan would win the NBA Finals MVP that year.

Since then, "Timmy" became the alpha male in the Spurs even though David Robinson was still manning the middle. The way Robinson deferred to the younger future Hall-of-Famer was also what Gregg Popovich wanted to see in his older players. Knowing when to hand over the reins was a trait that Robinson handed down to Timmy and one that the Big Fundamental would later pass on to guys like Tony Parker and Kawhi Leonard. It was attitude above talent, and it was a credo that a crucial element in his players for Pop.

For Robinson, he did not mind handing the keys to Tim Duncan since the Spurs were winning and it was clear that they were playing remarkably well under Pop's leadership and system.

The Spurs would find continued success in the next season, though they would fail to repeat as champions. Employing the same defensive style, Popovich had the Spurs playing at the fifth-slowest pace in the league. Nevertheless, they were first concerning points given to the other team while ranking fifth in terms of opponents' field goal percentage. It was a mirror of what Gregg Popovich wanted to see from the Olympic team back in 1972. He wanted them to play with less flash and more defense. That was exactly what the Spurs did in the early stages of Gregg Popovich's leadership. While the Lakers ended up winning three straight titles from 2000 to 2002, Popovich's Spurs maintained their status as contenders and challengers to the dominant Los Angeles team during those rivalry years.

The Formation of the Big Three

Sometime in the late 1990s, Avery Johnson, the Spurs' starting point guard, recalled how Gregg Popovich took him into the film room one day and made him watch a video of a shaggy-haired teenager that played outside the United States. Pop told him that they were planning to draft that teenager once he declared himself eligible for the NBA Draft. Then, after drafting him, he wanted to stash away that teenager and allow him to develop against international competition. That kid turned out to be Manu Ginóbili.[ii] The Spurs ended up drafting him in 1999 shortly after winning the championship. True to Pop's words, they would allow Manu to grow and evolve in Argentina and several other international basketball leagues before signing him in 2002.

Manu would eventually become one of the premier shooting guards in the league. He had all the talent in the world to challenge guys like Kobe Bryant, Tracy McGrady, and Vince Carter as one of the best shooting guards of his generation. Despite that, Manu was content with playing within a Spurs system that utilized his ability to score in bunches off the bench as the third option of a team that relied more on teamwork than on "hero ball" and isolation plays. Had he played as a starter and as the top option for another team, Manu Ginóbili may have had better numbers, but he would not have won the titles he won or garners the same respect that came with them.

Back in 2001, 36-year-old Avery Johnson moved to Denver, and the San Antonio Spurs were left without a starting point guard that knew the system. While their front line was thick, the Spurs had a weak point-guard rotation coming into the following season. However, during the offseason that year, R. C. Buford convinced Gregg Popovich to give a 19-year-old Frenchman named Tony Parker a shot after seeing him dominate the competition in France.[v]

At first, Popovich was skeptical about the teenager from France. He had never seen or heard about Tony Parker before, so Buford asked him to give the kid a workout. He would nevertheless accede to his close friend's request and had Parker fly 12 hours from France to San Antonio for a workout. The assignment that Pop gave to his scout was simple. He told him to get physical with the young kid and hound him the entire workout.

Tony Parker admitted that he had one of his worst performances during that workout. Parker struggled against the tough and tight defense that his matchup put on him. That was what Gregg Popovich was watching for—he wanted how Tony Parker would respond to the much more physical brand of basketball in the NBA.

Sadly, the young teenager did not live up to expectations. Pop was not impressed. He told Buford, who claimed that Parker was going to be the point guard of the future for the Spurs, that the Frenchman was nothing like he had described. Being the honest man that he was, he told Tony Parker that they were not going to draft him even after having him fly over to the States just for a workout.

Parker took the opportunity to work out with other teams. Over the course of the next few weeks, Tony Parker had impressed several coaches enough that they considered drafting him. And because of how well Parker performed in several workouts, word reached Gregg Popovich, who was finally convinced to give the kid another shot.

Tony Parker blew the head coach's mind in his second workout. Parker would later attribute his bad performance in his first workout to jet lag and fatigue from the 12-hour flight. Come draft day, San Antonio took the gamble and used their pick to bring in the 19-year-old kid from France.

Tony Parker had a respectable rookie season after immediately becoming the team's starting point guard. He admitted that he had rough patches, especially with how Pop was so hard on him. Plus, Timmy never even spoke a word to him that rookie year, but Parker worked harder every single season to become an All-Star point guard and to earn the respect of his teammates.

That was the origin story of how the Spurs' Big Three was formed. Gregg Popovich went on to coach the legendary players to become the winningest trio in league history. Since 2002, the trio of Tim Duncan, Manu Ginóbili, and Tony Parker seemed inseparable and was the model group of teammates for any roster out there, much like how the Spurs were the modern organization to emulate. They were not the closest of friends and did not hang out with each other often but, on the court, they knew their roles and each other's tendencies down to a letter. The chemistry in that Big Three was so clear that it did not matter who was going to take the last shot or who was going to be the focal point of the offensive attack. They just *clicked* and it was a joy to watch.

How Gregg Popovich managed to get the trio to work together for over a decade with consistency and excellence all boiled down to how the head coach valued the players' attitude and traits above their individual skills and athleticism. As a player, Popovich was never about being big, athletic, or skillful. He played with intensity and used his basketball IQ while never forgetting to make the right passes and take the shots he knew he could make. He worked harder than anyone else on the floor. He was looking for a mirror of himself when looking at players he thought were fit to become members of the San Antonio Spurs organization.

In an interview, Gregg Popovich said that what the team always looked at first was the player's character. But character had always been a subjective trait. For Pop, a player with the right character was someone who had gotten over his individual self and had grown up to look at the bigger picture. Popovich knew whether the player had that kind of a trait just by talking to them. He wanted someone that understood that he was just a piece of a larger puzzle instead of looking at himself as the centerpiece. And of course, he would also say that having a sense of humor did not hurt.[vi]

Pop also stated that he wanted players that were already comfortable with who they were and what they provided for the team. No single player has the answer to everything. Michael Jordan needed Scottie Pippen and his teammates. Kobe Bryant and Shaquille O'Neal needed each other. LeBron James needed fellow All-Stars on his team. That was what Gregg Popovich wanted his players to understand. Everybody is just a piece of a larger puzzle. There was no room for inflated egos. They are participatory characters in the larger scheme of things instead of being the entire show itself. That was a trait Pop wanted his players to have.[iv]

Being the stern disciplinarian and straightforward man that he was, Gregg Popovich also looked for players that knew how to handle feedback and criticism. He treated his players equally. Tim Duncan was treated just the same as every guy parked on the bench. Even Timmy got scolded when he was not doing what he was asked to do. The ability to listen and take information objectively was a quality Pop and his coaching staff looked for, and not just in the United States but also overseas as well.

Consistent Contenders

A year after drafting Tony Parker, Manu Ginóbili became the final linchpin of what would become the Big Three when he finally signed with the team. Manu did not have the best rookie season but was good enough as an option off the bench for a dominant San Antonio Spurs team that won 60 games. They were the best team in a tough Western Conference that year.

It was during that 2002-03 season when Tim Duncan was awarded the second of his back-to-back MVP awards. He had grown to become the league's best power forward and possibly even the best player in the NBA. Parker began owning his role as starting point guard and secondary scorer to Timmy. Bruce Bowen, who was considered their most valuable player on the defensive end, was owning his role in stopping the other team's best player. Even the 37-year-old David Robinson was doing his best to help the team win. It was a team of players that knew and played their roles to perfection. With the way Gregg Popovich led his team both on and off the court, it was no wonder why he won his first Coach of the Year Award that season.

Come playoff time, San Antonio finally ended the Los Angeles' Lakers three-year run as titleholders by eliminating them in the second round in six games. Having beaten the three-time champions, it was only right for them to reach the NBA Finals and cap off another great run for the title. They beat the New Jersey Nets in six games to become the 2003 NBA Champions.

For both Gregg Popovich and Tim Duncan, they were celebrating the second of what was going to be five titles. Both Tony Parker and Manu Ginóbili were champions for the first time in their NBA careers. And for David Robinson, he would retire at the end of the season as a two-time NBA champion under the tutelage and leadership of Gregg Popovich, whom he had worked with for nearly the entirety of his NBA career.

While Popovich and his San Antonio Spurs failed to repeat as champions during the 2003-04 season, they would come back stronger than ever the following season wherein Pop was named head coach of the Western All-Star team for the first time in his career. With 59 wins under his belt that season, he would once again lead the Spurs to a strong outing in the playoffs where they dominated the Western Conference to claim another appearance in the NBA Finals.

In the NBA Finals that year, the Spurs faced their formidable counterparts in the Eastern Conference. Gregg Popovich would meet his former mentor and close friend Larry Brown, who coached the Detroit Pistons that season. The Spurs and the Pistons were nearly mirrors of each other back then, considering the similar background of their head coaches and the same slow-paced defensive style they played. There is no doubt that both Popovich and Brown thought and strategized alike in many ways—once upon a time, they had each learned a lot from the other.

Both teams played a slow-paced style that focused more on suffocating defense. The San Antonio Spurs were 23rd in terms of pace that season. Meanwhile, the Pistons were dead last. Moreover, San Antonio held their opponents to a league-low 88.4 points per game that season. Detroit was second to the Spurs in points scored by the opposing team, holding their opponents to 89.5 points per game.

The 2005 NBA Finals was not only a battle between the two best defensive teams of that era but also a friendly rivalry between two of the brightest coaching minds in the world. The series was hard-fought on both sides and went all the way to Game 7, where Gregg Popovich and his Spurs ultimately managed to triumph over the Pistons and the man that had helped him get to the NBA. Despite the fierce battle between their teams, Pop's relationship with his former mentor was never tarnished. The two remained good friends even when Gregg Popovich went on to win his third NBA title—three out of three trips—to the Finals.

The following season, the San Antonio Spurs were again on top of the NBA food chain during the regular season. The team's slow-paced defensive style still dominated the NBA and gave opposing teams nightmares. What was even scarier was that the core trio of Tim Duncan, Tony Parker, and Manu Ginóbili were all playing in the prime of their respective careers and dominating the league, despite playing limited minutes in a squad that focused on team play.

Ever the fearsome squad, the Spurs won 63 games that season. They won over the Sacramento Kings in the first round of the playoffs before going up against the Dallas Mavericks in the second round. That was when Pop had to face another familiar friend who sat on the bench of the opposing team.

At a young age, Pop's former starting point guard, Avery Johnson, was already coaching a contending Dallas Mavericks team. Johnson learned the ins and outs of coaching in the several seasons he spent under

Pop's wing as a player. He would put that experience to good use against his mentor. Much like how Pop felled his own mentor, Larry Brown, a year before in the Finals, Johnson would beat Gregg Popovich's San Antonio Spurs in seven games to eventually reach the championship round. While Pop might have failed to repeat as a champion, it was still an immensely proud moment for Pop to see one of his former students, especially one whom he had believed in and cultivated for so many years, succeeding as a head coach. Some things in life were bigger than basketball itself.

Heading into the 2006-07 season, the San Antonio Spurs stayed true to their slow-paced roots and were still the most dominant and consistent team in the Western Conference—an amazing ten years from the time that Gregg Popovich took over the team's role as the head coach. Using their smothering defense and championship experience, they would breeze through the Western Conference playoff picture and lost only four games heading into the NBA Finals.

For the third straight season, Popovich would once again meet a familiar face at the other end of the court: Mike Brown. Brown first started working as a coach in 2000 when Pop hired him as an assistant for the Spurs and he stayed with the team until 2003 when they won a title. He then moved over to Indiana before becoming the head coach of the Cleveland Cavaliers in 2005.

There was an interesting story involving the two coaches. Back in 2002 when Brown was still working as an assistant for Pop, the future Cavaliers head coach was struggling with some personal arrangements between him and his ex-wife. Their kids stayed with Brown's ex-wife, but would often visit him in San Antonio. One day, Brown's sister brought his two sons to San Antonio to visit him. They cried hard when it was time to leave.

During that incident, Mike Brown called Gregg Popovich to inform him that he would be running late because of family matters he had to first take care of. He told his coach that he might arrive a little later than usual to the team plane when the Spurs were about to travel to Chicago for a road game. But Pop told his assistant to miss the plane, the trip, and the game to let him focus on the family matter he had at hand. He even threatened to fire Mike Brown if he caught up with the team. Of course, Brown decided to stay with his kids that day.[ii] As strict and harsh a disciplinarian as Pop was, he knew how much more important family was. That was another important value that he imparted not only to his players but also to his assistants and staff as well.

Going back to 2007, Mike Brown tried to lead his Cavaliers to victory by harnessing the otherworldly skills of LeBron James, who would soon become the best player on the planet. But Brown stood no chance against his mentor, who would lead the San Antonio Spurs to a clean four-game sweep in the Finals on his way to a perfect 4-0 record in the championship series.

With that win, Gregg Popovich clinched his fourth NBA title ring. Pop had achieved true greatness as a coach, fame, and fortune at that point in his career, but he still managed to stay grounded and humble despite all the success he was blessed with.

Popovich and his San Antonio Spurs continued to be one of the top contenders for the NBA title in the 2007-08 season as the defending champions. However, they were not spared from criticism. The team that Pop was coaching was getting older and could no longer keep up as well with the fresh, young legs of Western Conference teams that loved running. Among the 14 players that played at least 20 games for the Spurs that season, only Tony Parker and Matt Bonner were less than 30 years old. The other role players like Brent Barry, Bruce Bowen, and Kurt Thomas were already elder statesmen in the league.

Despite the advanced age of most of his key players, Gregg Popovich was still able to get his team to fight as strong contenders by continuing to play a slow-paced game. That trademark slow pace suited the style of his players and helped nullify any youth advantage that opposing teams had. However, what was important to Pop was the wisdom and experience that his older veterans brought to the team. These were players that had bounced around from squad to squad in their respective careers and had already grown in character and experience. Banking on that, Pop was able to lead the Spurs to a 56-26 record during the regular season.

In the first round, San Antonio would breeze past the Phoenix Suns, whom they had formed a rivalry with over the past few seasons due to the stark contrast in the way the two vastly different teams played the game. The Spurs still favored a slow game while the Suns ran the floor whenever they could. But the Suns could never figure out Gregg Popovich and lost the series, 1-4.

The Spurs faced a tougher matchup in the second round when they came up against a young Chris Paul leading an upstart New Orleans Hornets team. The Hornets managed to force the series to seven games, but experience won out in the end and the San Antonio Spurs were on their way to the Western Conference Finals and a chance to qualify for the NBA Finals once again.

The Western Conference Finals that season was a battle between two of the best coaching minds in the history of the NBA. Phil Jackson of the Los Angeles Lakers was gunning for a record-breaking 10th NBA title. And while Pop was still a long way from tying or breaking any records, he had been the man at the helm of the league's most consistent franchise since 1997.

Unfortunately for Pop, youth and speed triumphed as the Lakers defeated the Spurs in five games. For the fourth time, the Spurs failed to defend their title in the

NBA Finals after once again falling short of reaching the championship series.

The next two seasons were perceived as struggling years for a consistent franchise like the San Antonio Spurs, despite the team winning at least 50 games. Age had caught up with the roster and their slow-paced style was no longer working in a league that was transitioning into one that favored a faster pace and the three-point shot. Some were even claiming that Gregg Popovich's style had become obsolete and that his key players were no longer good enough to lead the team back to championship contention. The same thing happened to the Pistons, who entered a rebuilding stage after their slow-paced style had failed. Perhaps it was inevitable that the fast-paced teams would eventually learn to counteract that slow-paced style, and the rise of the three-point shot was a key element in that change. The Spurs would bow out of the playoffs early in those two seasons.

The Transition, Acquiring Kawhi Leonard

Tim Duncan had grown too old to be the centerpiece of Gregg Popovich's offense, though he was still more than capable of putting up All-Star numbers. The role players he used to rely on in the previous seasons had either moved over to other teams or retired due to their advanced age. And what was clear was that the slow-paced defensive style of basketball that Pop had been employing since 1997 was no longer working like it used to.

But Gregg Popovich, ever the visionary, had long prepared for the moment when his style would no longer work and when his veteran role players had grown too old or retired. He had begun to employ younger role players that nobody else in the league seemingly wanted. Big man DeJuan Blair had a lot of red flags because he did not have any cartilage in either of his knees. George Hill, whom the team had acquired a few seasons back, was a promising backup point guard that could start for any other team, but he never fell on any other team's radar. Shooters Gary Neal and Danny Green had struggled on their previous teams but found a home in San Antonio because they played their role as outside threats well enough.

With younger role players surrounding the Big Three in San Antonio, Gregg Popovich would hand the keys of the offense to Tony Parker in what would become a faster San Antonio Spurs team. Parker became the centerpiece of an offense that used to rely principally on Tim Duncan, who would play less than 30 minutes for the first time in his career that season as part of Pop's strategy to conserve the legs of the man regarded as the best power forward in league history.

The faster pace worked for the San Antonio Spurs, who suddenly jumped to the fifth-highest scoring team in the league that season. And they did it without any of their players playing more than 33 minutes a night or averaging more than 20 points per game. It was a style that was predicated on ball movement and looking for the best available shot. San Antonio would surprise everyone and win 61 games during the regular season to headline the Western Conference as the top-seeded team in the playoffs.

Nobody expected such a drastic change from a team that had been playing a slow-paced style for nearly a decade and a half. The team kept the same key roster members but added role players that fit the new system. They did not even change the coaching staff or the personnel that came with it. More amazingly, the San Antonio Spurs did not undergo a rebuilding process that would have had them losing more games than they won. It was a smooth transition from what was the slowest paced team since 1997 to what would become a fast team that relied on three-point shots and ball movement. How Gregg Popovich did it almost seemed unbelievable. It was a season that showcased not only the venerable coach's wisdom but also a surprising adaptability as he tailored his coaching style to mesh with the new faster-paced playing style of the NBA.

However, the San Antonio Spurs would see a mirror image of their former selves in the first round of the playoffs. The Memphis Grizzlies, who employed a similar slow-paced grind-it-out style that the Spurs used to run but still had age in their favor. The Grizzlies used their grit to force the Spurs offense into difficult situations. Pop and his Spurs were ultimately thwarted by the defensive style of the Grizzlies, who managed to pull off a monumental upset by winning the series against the top-seeded team in the Western Conference.

The San Antonio Spurs were never one-hit wonders that would suddenly fade into obscurity the next season after having a successful campaign a year before. Popovich always made sure that the Spurs were consistent and hungry for a title year in and year out, even after experiencing something as devastating and unexpected as losing to the eighth-seeded team in the playoffs. Moreover, he would not second-guess himself or the changes he had set in motion, or derail the progress the team had achieved by playing a faster-paced game. Instead, Pop would stay on course and continue the same system while focusing more on his guards' abilities.

In what was initially a surprising step for Gregg Popovich and the San Antonio Spurs, who seldom traded young and productive players, a move was made involving backup point guard George Hill. Hill had proven himself as a bright backup guard playing with Tony Parker in his first three seasons in San Antonio. He played defense perfectly while knowing the Spurs' offense by heart. But Pop had his eye on another gem in the 20-year-old draft hopeful, Kawhi Leonard.

Kawhi Leonard played forward for two years at San Diego State before trying his hand in the NBA Draft. The problem with Kawhi as a prospect was that he had no particular set of skills that stood out. He was physically gifted. Standing at 6'7", weighing 230 pounds of lean muscle, and sporting large hands and long arms, Leonard was a great athletic specimen. However, this gem was unpolished—he was raw. He did not have a go-to move in college. His outside shooting was awful. All he had with him were his athletic and physical attributes.

But Gregg Popovich saw something special in the young man. He was unique enough for Pop to give away a proven and improving backup point guard in exchange for a rookie that was a gamble. The Indiana Pacers would draft him 15th overall in the 2011 NBA Draft but would give him up to the Spurs in exchange for George Hill.

In Kawhi Leonard, Popovich saw the makings of a franchise star, but not because he was dominant in college or because he already had a particular set of skills and talents that only needed development. It was because he saw the same core characteristics he had seen and valued in Tim Duncan, Tony Parker, and

Manu Ginóbili more than a decade before. Leonard was every bit a match to what Pop wanted in a player on the Spurs' roster.

Kawhi Leonard was simple, humble, and discreet. His quiet demeanor belied his hunger to become one of the best players in the league. He understood his role with the team when he first came to the NBA. Gregg Popovich took him in initially to become a defender at the small forward position, a spot the San Antonio Spurs had troubles filling ever since Bruce Bowen's retirement. But he was meant for greater things than simply being Bowen 2.0.

Kawhi Leonard would bide his time developing in his speed and pace while contributing as a role player to the San Antonio Spurs' cause in his rookie season. Pop used the young rookie as a defender while the offense ran through Tony Parker and a Tim Duncan that had seemingly found the fountain of youth that season. The

San Antonio Spurs won 50 out of the 66 games they played in a lockout-shortened NBA season that year.

Without even using any player other than Tony Parker more than 30 minutes a night, Gregg Popovich led the San Antonio Spurs to the NBA's best record. He had his team playing the seventh-fastest pace while scoring the second-most points per game in the entire league, though only three of his players averaged more than 10 points per game. He had shown the league what perfect team basketball was all about.

Almost everything about the Spurs that season contrasted with the style the team was so used to just a few seasons back. San Antonio not only played at a fast pace but also favored shooting more three-pointers. The Spurs ranked seventh in the league in most three-pointers attempted per game and would rank second concerning shots made from that distance. They also ranked first regarding three-point shooting percentage. However, what was surprising was that Pop did not rely on his main core players to shoot the three-pointers. It was the role players like Gary Neal and Danny Green, who were once thought of as outcasts in the league, who shot and made three-pointers in bunches. Their contributions were the perfect example of how Pop favored a system that relied more on team basketball than individual skills.

Gregg Popovich would lead the San Antonio Spurs to a dominating performance in the playoffs. They quickly swept the Utah Jazz in the first round before doing the same to the Los Angeles Clippers in the Western Conference Semis. The Spurs would next meet a young, upstart Oklahoma City Thunder team that had three promising future superstars among their ranks.

The Oklahoma City Thunder core of Kevin Durant, Russell Westbrook, and James Harden were all drafted by a man who had roots with the San Antonio Spurs organization. While Thunder GM Sam Presti did not work directly under Gregg Popovich, he was, in fact, one of R. C. Buford's interns back in 2001. (Buford, Pop's good friend and long-time assistant, was the man that urged Pop to draft Tony Parker.)

Back in the 2012 Western Conference Finals, Gregg Popovich looked like he was on his way to another clean sweep after leading a dominating Spurs team to a 2-0 start to the series. However, the Thunder bounced back by using their young legs to run the Spurs down to the ground. They won four straight games to edge out San Antonio and make it to the NBA Finals, where they would ultimately lose to the Miami Heat.

While Gregg Popovich might have fallen short of making it back to the NBA Finals for the first time since 2007, the biggest positive he could take from that season was the fact that his Spurs had mastered the system he had wanted them to run. The Spurs ran a beautiful system that almost rivaled an orchestra because of how smooth and crisp their performances were. Moreover, the team had the ball moving like a hot potato, which was why they were fourth in the league in assists per game.

Return to the Finals, Fifth NBA Championship

After facing another disappointing setback the previous season, Gregg Popovich and his Spurs came back strong once again to try and dominate their way to a Finals return. Pop employed the same fast-paced ball movement that made the San Antonio Spurs so entertaining to watch in the past few seasons. Not only were they entertaining but they were also making themselves look like the model basketball team that any squad would want to emulate.

Popovich continued to preach ball movement to his team. The San Antonio Spurs ranked first in assists that season, mainly due to the way the players made extra passes like it was second nature to them. Nobody took a shot that did not have a chance to make it through the hoop. Everyone on the team moved the ball around until they found the most open man under the basket or outside the three-point area.

Pop would also show how fluid of a team the San Antonio Spurs were from their top guy all the way to the man at the deepest end of the bench by resting starters from time to time to preserve their legs for the playoffs or to boost his role players' confidence. The Spurs' Big Three did not even play over 70 games that season though their numbers remained mostly the same. Tony Parker was still the alpha gun as he averaged over 20 points and nearly 8 assists that season. Meanwhile, at the advanced age of 36, Tim Duncan was norming 18 points, 10 rebounds, and almost 3 blocks while playing 30 minutes a night. It was a team built to dominate and win the title that season.

Though Pop made it a habit to rest his starters, especially during tight schedules, the San Antonio Spurs still managed to win 58 games during the regular season to secure the second seed in the Western Conference. They quickly dispatched the Los Angeles Lakers in the first round before seeing a valiant but futile fight from an upstart young Golden State Warriors team, who they beat in six games. And in the Western Conference Finals, the San Antonio Spurs reaped sweet revenge over their humiliating loss two seasons ago by sweeping the Grizzlies in four games. It would mark both Gregg Popovich's and Tim Duncan's fifth Finals appearance since 1999.

Gunning for his fifth championship ring, Pop led his San Antonio Spurs against a dominant and daunting Miami Heat team that was composed of three superstars in the prime of their careers. He traded wins and losses with the Heat during that difficult series until it reached a pivotal Game 6 where the San Antonio Spurs were seemingly about to win the franchise's fifth championship trophy.

The San Antonio Spurs were leading by five points with just seconds left when LeBron James of the Heat hit a three-pointer to cut the deficit down to two. The ball came back to the Spurs and Miami immediately fouled the second-year forward, Kawhi Leonard, when the ball found its way into his hands. The Finals jitters got to young Leonard, who only made half of his free throws. Then, on the other end, Miami's Ray Allen tied the game with another three-pointer to send it to overtime, where Miami eventually won. The Heat then won Game 7. It was Gregg Popovich's first loss in the NBA Finals.

After that loss, Pop met with Duncan, Parker, and Ginóbili. The three players had given him his last three championship rings. Together, they questioned if that was the end of their run. "Was that the best they could do?" they wondered. Popovich even contemplated retiring that season because he wondered if the competitive spirit was still with them.[vii]

However, after weeks of questioning themselves, Pop and all of the Big Three decided to return. Duncan held off retirement once more. Ginóbili re-signed with the team to prove he was not yet done. Parker decided to lead the team once more towards a title run.

Pop challenged the trio of stars and did the same with the other guys. He made them watch the Game 6 loss over and over again until they all moved on and realized they could not do anything about it anymore. All that did was challenge them even more and try to fix the mistakes that led to that hurtful loss to the Heat during the 2013 NBA Finals.[vii]

Teams do not typically come back from a Finals loss the next season looking like they had forgotten how devastating the defeat was, or just how close they had come to a championship. But Gregg Popovich taught his team to have a short memory. There was nothing they could do about that loss. The only thing the Spurs could do was to come back hungrier and stronger. That was what Pop did with the 2013-14 San Antonio Spurs, which would eventually become one of the best teams in league history.

If ever there was a model team of excellence in the history of the NBA, it would be that season's San Antonio Spurs. Gregg Popovich relentlessly taught them the value of teamwork and ball movement. At one or more points during the regular season, even the role players looked like All-Stars. Pop never played anyone more than 30 minutes a night that season. Tim Duncan, Manu Ginóbili, Kawhi Leonard, and even Tony Parker all played under 30 minutes per game, yet the Spurs still managed to dominate a tough Western Conference landscape by playing basketball the right way.

San Antonio would lead the league during the regular season by winning 62 games even though Pop regularly rested his main guys. Nobody could quite figure out just how Gregg Popovich was doing it. He was making role players look like borderline stars. Even the forgotten guys like Boris Diaw found a way to rejuvenate their careers in San Antonio. The Spurs looked better and better every season because Pop was perfecting his model system that most championship teams follow today.

Despite the brilliance they displayed during the regular season, the Spurs would face a tough first-round battle against the eighth-seeded Dallas Mavericks, who almost defeated them in seven games. Come the second round, San Antonio routed the Portland Trail Blazers in five games before meeting the Thunder again in the Conference Finals. But this time, the Spurs had their number and would win all of their home games to beat OKC in six games and to return to the NBA Finals for a second consecutive time. That season also marked Gregg Popovich's first time to make back-to-back NBA Finals appearances.

The 2014 NBA Finals was a rematch between the Spurs and the Heat. This time, however, it looked nothing like their fierce battle of a year before. In what was considered one of the most lopsided NBA Finals ever played, the Spurs defeated the Heat in five games. All four of their wins came by double digits as San Antonio ran the ball around the Miami defense to perfection.

The 2014 NBA Finals was also a landmark series for Gregg Popovich when it came to coaching. When the San Antonio Spurs lost Game 2 to the Miami Heat, he found a way to neutralize the best player on the planet by looking towards the young man that was partly the reason for why they lost Game 6 a year before.

Kawhi Leonard was fresh off a season averaging 12 points per game but was still primarily a defender. Pop gave him the most unenviable task in the NBA— guarding and shutting down LeBron James. Instead, in the first two games, Leonard was shut down and would only combine for 18 points. That Game 2 loss was what turned things around.

After Game 2, Pop had a talk with his third-year future star. He told Kawhi Leonard to forget about Parker, Duncan, and Ginóbili because *he* had become the star of the team. He urged his long-armed forward to shoot the ball more and compete harder than he had ever done in his life. Kawhi Leonard responded by going for 29, 20, and 22 points respectively in the next three games to cap off a spectacular 2014 run for the Spurs. Leonard averaged nearly 18 points and shot over 60% during the Finals thanks largely in part to how Pop handed the offense down to him during that series.

Gregg Popovich's incredible instinct and strategic genius were what led the Spurs to their remarkable 2014 NBA Finals victory. He had figured out how to turn the Miami Heat's strengths into weaknesses. The Heat relied a lot on how aggressive they were in playing the passing lanes on defense. If they made a small mistake on a pass, James or Wade would pick it off and convert it into a transition slam over at the other end a few seconds later.

But Popovich cleverly turned that maneuver around on them. He knew how fast the Miami Heat were at playing the passing lanes. So, what he did was make his players make the pass even quicker than how the Heat players were reacting to them. No player in the history of the league has ever been faster with the ball when it came down to passes. Pop knew that and exploited it the best that he could. He made his team pass the ball around quicker than any team has ever done in the history of the team to tire the Heat out while making sure his players were finding the most open shots.

Gregg Popovich would call that strategy "Summertime" because it was just like playing in your local park during summer.[vii] There were no direct instructions. It was fundamental basketball at its finest.

You passed the ball around until it hit an open man. And when that man found a more open man in the half-second differential between him and a Miami Heat player recovering on defense, his teammate got a better shot than he did. Pop made sure nobody touched the ball more than half a second because that was how quick the Heat defenders could recover. It was using fundamental play against a team designed to disrupt strategy. Pop used the Heat's strengths against them. That was how the genius of Gregg Popovich worked.

Think of it this way. The Miami Heat at that time did not exactly play man-to-man defense every single player and had mixed man-to-man with a zone type of defense so that it would be easier for their athletes to jump the passing lanes or to disrupt offenses that were too slow to rotate the ball around. At the moment a player finally decided on an action with the ball, seconds after receiving a pass, multiple Heat defenders would be ready to converge on him and pressure the ball if he tried to drive to the basket. And when he finally decided to give the ball up, after realizing there was no way for him to score, the Heat defenders had already recovered to the weak side.

In that regard, Gregg Popovich found a way to circumvent that by making sure that his players were passing the ball around before they could even decide what to do with the ball in their hands. This allowed multiple Heat defenders to keep on recovering and converging to whoever had the ball. But because the ball will always move faster than any defensive player, there will eventually be an open man near the basket or outside the three-point line after the defenders failed to recover to the weak side in time.

This type of offense eventually became one of the models of success for future NBA teams, as the game eventually learned to rely more on ball movement and pace-and-space. It was all thanks to Gregg Popovich's pioneering, prototype offense he worked in that 2014 championship run.

And while the San Antonio Spurs failed to defend their championship the following season, the innovative way they had played that 2014 NBA Finals had a lasting impact on the game of basketball that was much more profound than a mere championship win. Gregg Popovich had literally changed the game and his influence had created a ripple effect throughout the NBA that was beginning to resonate. Two teams started to look like the San Antonio Spurs of 2014. The 2014-15 Atlanta Hawks, coached by a former Popovich assistant, Mike Budenholzer, led the team to 60 wins. He had four All-Stars on a team that played team ball very effectively. Role player Kyle Korver was even selected as an All-Star because of how effective the Hawks played that brand of basketball.

And even more effective at that brand of basketball were the Stephen Curry-led Golden State Warriors coached by Steve Kerr, who had played for Gregg Popovich for a few seasons back in the early 2000s. He and Warriors' GM Bob Myers also watched the 2014

NBA Finals keenly and were amazed at how Gregg Popovich easily made the Heat look like local YMCA players because of the ball movement he employed.

The Warriors became a mirror of that Spurs team but were arguably better thanks to their youth and how their top shooters were better than the ones that Popovich had in that 2014 title run. Golden State would go on to dominate their way towards three NBA championships in a span of just four years by taking what the Spurs did in 2014 and making it better. They led the league with 67 wins during the 2014-15 regular season and even broke a league record with 73 wins a year later. They were usually at the top in terms of pace, points per game, field goal percentage, and assists, precisely because of the similar kind of ball movement and fluidity they took out of Pop's playbook.

Several other teams followed suit by playing the game faster and moving the ball with more fluidity while looking for three-pointers or inside incursions. That was the lasting effect that Gregg Popovich had on the league. He focused on the core essentials of basketball and improved upon it.

In the blink of an eye, Pop's innovation became an evolving trend until every other team in the league thought they were the 2014 San Antonio Spurs. But the Spurs would soon change their identity and evolve in a new direction once again, just when all the other teams were trying to *be* them. This illustrates one of the greatest things of all about the game of basketball—it is always changing, always evolving. No two eras are ever the same. Popovich's eagerly-adopted strategy will someday be just a footnote in the annals of league history as the game continues to reinvent itself.

The Rise of Kawhi Leonard, Tim Duncan's Retirement

The way Gregg Popovich molded role players into great rotation contributors and how he developed a system of equal opportunity for everyone in the team made San Antonio an ideal hotbed for free agents, even though the Spurs were playing in a small market. Veterans David West, Kevin Martin, and Andre Miller made their way to the team. More importantly, they were able to win the free agency jackpot when they signed LaMarcus Aldridge, who was one of the best power forwards the league had to offer at that time.

The presence of another towering figure and the emergence of Kawhi Leonard as an All-Star led Popovich to make another change in the Spurs' system. The team would actually go back to their roots of playing a slower-paced style that focused more on defense. However, it was an entirely different system from when Tim Duncan was still in his prime. Instead of looking for a post player inside the paint, Pop had his team playing the same kind of unselfish ball that would consistently look for the best available shot in a slow-paced system. The focus was on finding open men on the perimeter and inside the paint instead of the three-point area.

The latest system worked wonders for the San Antonio Spurs and was the perfect complement to Kawhi Leonard's skills. The crisp ball movement they played with from 2011 to 2014, combined with the slow-paced defensive style they used to dominate the league during the 2000s, resulted in what was possibly Gregg Popovich's best system of all. The Spurs led the league in defensive rating while allowing the lowest points per game on the part of their opponents. And despite being the seventh-slowest team in the league concerning pace, the Spurs' offense was not affected. They still ranked 10th in the league in points per game. They were also fourth in offensive rating. It was the

2014 Spurs' offensive fluidity coupled with the 2003 Spurs' defensive mastery. And it was brilliant.

The San Antonio Spurs returned to their dominant ways that season and would have been the best in the league had the Golden State Warriors not won 73 regular-season games that season. Had Popovich not rested his starters and key players, they might have challenged the Warriors' regular-season record. But they settled for second best during the regular season with a franchise record of 67 wins.

But after dominating the Memphis Grizzlies in the first round of the playoffs to complete a sweep, the Spurs met a hungry Oklahoma City Thunder that was peaking at the right time. The Thunder superstar duo of Kevin Durant and Russell Westbrook were entering the prime of their respective careers and looked even hungrier than the Spurs. San Antonio ended up losing the series in six games to finish what was their best regular season in franchise history.

Their matchup against the OKC Thunder in the 2016 Playoffs also revealed one of the Spurs' biggest weaknesses that season: Tim Duncan's age. Just a few seasons prior, Gregg Popovich had Duncan looking like he was 29 again. But the 39-year-old veteran had suffered an injury that slowed him down drastically and exposed the wear-and-tear of 19 hard-fought seasons.

After that season, Tim Duncan realized that he could no longer take the grind of another 82-game season and decided to retire in silent fashion, much the same way he had quietly and unassumingly dominated the league for nearly two decades. Duncan's retirement ended a relationship of excellence he had had with Gregg Popovich since 1997. He had given his head coach five NBA titles in a span of 19 seasons. And as for Pop, he wanted nothing less than a player of the same caliber and mindset as Duncan. Pop, in fact, had since looked for a player with the same demeanor and humility that Timmy had but with a deep-seated hunger for greatness that still needed to be uncovered—and he believed that he had found just such a player. The man to whom Gregg Popovich and the entire organization looked upon to lead them the same way as Tim Duncan had was Kawhi Leonard, who was an All-Star for the first time in 2016 and had become one of the most elite players in 2017.

But while Leonard's development into the premier two-way player of the league was the biggest story of the San Antonio Spurs during the 2016-17 season, the team would not have achieved another 60-win season had Pop not also attracted the likes of Pau Gasol and David Lee during free agency. Another lesson Pop never forgot was the long-ago wisdom involving David Robinson: you never put all your eggs in one basket or allowed your team to hinge upon just one person.

The Spurs' first season since Tim Duncan's retirement showcased how well anyone with a selfless mentality and hunger to win games in a team setup would fit with Pop's system. Lee rejuvenated his career in San Antonio while Pau Gasol did not look like he was even remotely close to 36 years old. Nobody was even surprised at how the Spurs were still tops in defensive rating while finishing top 10 in offensive rating towards a 61-21 record in the regular season. After all, they had Pop.

Nevertheless, the top man of that team was now Kawhi Leonard, who had blossomed into a true NBA superstar following the retirement of Tim Duncan. Leonard, however, would suffer an injury during the Western Conference Finals when the Warriors' Zaza Pachulia stepped under him after a shot attempt. This injury not only sabotaged the Spurs' amazing season that year but it also eventually led to a falling out between Kawhi Leonard and Gregg Popovich the following year.

The End of the 20-Year Dynasty of Excellence

During the 2017-18 season, the San Antonio Spurs fell under the 60% winning percentage mark for the first time since the 1997-98 season, as Kawhi Leonard was still dealing with his injury issues. The injuries made him want to leave San Antonio due to how he felt that Popovich mishandled his injury problems by having him play and train in certain stretches that season. As the Spurs folded in the first round of the playoffs, the inevitable came to happen when they traded Kawhi Leonard to the Toronto Raptors in exchange for All-Star wing DeMar DeRozan. Following that trade, Popovich was vocal in saying that, while Kawhi Leonard was indeed a great player, he did not have the leadership skills he was hoping to get out of the league's best two-way player.[viii]

Popovich's comments about Leonard might have come from how he felt hurt but everything he said came from the heart. After all, for nearly two decades, Pop had learned to rely on players who stayed with the team regardless of whatever situation they were in. Duncan stayed. Ginóbili stayed. Parker stayed (even though he ended his final year in the league with the Charlotte Hornets). Meanwhile, even though Kawhi Leonard had the right to leave a situation he did not like, loyalty mattered to Gregg Popovich when it came to players he saw fit to lead his San Antonio Spurs.

After a 48-win season during the 2018-19 campaign, the San Antonio Spurs narrowly missed the 60% mark for winning percentage but were still competitive enough to make it to the playoffs, even though the team did not win 50 games under the Popovich leadership for two straight years already. But, even though the talents of Aldridge and DeRozan flourished, something changed in the Spurs' system as Gregg Popovich made it a point to stray away from the three-point line shot.

The 2018-19 San Antonio Spurs, even though they had won a title back in 2014 due partly to their reliance on the three-pointer, finished dead last in terms of three-point field-goal attempts. Meanwhile, they also became one of the slowest-paced teams in the league. But it was all by design as Gregg Popovich figured that most teams in that era were reluctant to guard the midrange shot due to how advanced analytics had revealed the fact that the three-point shot is far more efficient than any shot within the perimeter except for open layups in the painted area. The strategy did not work, however, as the Spurs were booted out of the playoffs in the first round once again.

As a man who openly admitted that he has always hated the three-point shot, even though he utilized it well enough at one point in his coaching career, Gregg Popovich still preached the importance of the midrange shot and of other shots closer to the basket during the 2019-20 season, wherein the Spurs were barely qualifying for a playoff spot. Even though the San Antonio Spurs were one of the teams invited to the "Orlando bubble" that came as a result of how the

NBA needed to stop games midway through March of 2020 due to the Coronavirus outbreak, the Spurs struggled in the restart and failed to make it to the playoffs for the first time since Popovich led them to the postseason in 1998.

For 22 years, the San Antonio Spurs under Gregg Popovich became the model organization in terms of consistency. Truth be told, they were not always the best team in those 22 years and were not always good enough to contend for titles. But what made them the model for consistency was the fact that they never had to go through rebuild seasons under Popovich but were still able to stay consistent and relevant in the NBA and even managed to win five titles in totally different eras.

However, things changed and time seemed to have left the Spurs floundering in the past as critics pointed to the fact that Gregg Popovich failed to embrace the three-point line because he felt like the shot was more

of a circus gimmick than an actual play in basketball.[ix]
His personal beliefs were what ultimately led to the
downfall of a successful franchise, as the Spurs did not
get with the times and failed to adjust accordingly to
an NBA that had evolved to embrace the three-point
line as the top weapon of choice.

Nevertheless, if there was something that stood out
about Popovich since he started coaching, it was that
he always found a way to succeed, no matter what the
circumstances were. Whether that will prove true of
Pop in the future is still up for debate but we certainly
will not be counting him out. Gregg Popovich may still
find his own special way to help his team get back on
track in the coming NBA seasons. And given his
incredible history as one of the greatest coaches of our
time, we would even go so far as to say that it is more
likely than not.

Chapter 4: The Gregg Popovich System

The Right Players

While skill, talent, and athletic abilities are what defines an NBA superstar, they are not necessarily what makes a player a champion in the league. For a championship coach such as Gregg Popovich, character has always been the most important trait when it came down to looking for the right personnel to fit the needs of his system and roster.

Popovich has always been proud of his innate ability to tell a person's character just by conversing with him. He does the same with players he hopes to give a spot on his roster. Pop claims that when a player seemingly always talks about himself and about what he needs from the team, he has not reached the selfless state that is required by the Spurs. Popovich focuses on players that have already given up their personal needs to contribute to the greater cause of the team.

Ever since the day he started coaching the San Antonio Spurs, Gregg Popovich had a good mix of veterans and young players that seemingly gelled together on the court. He knew how to maximize his veterans' experience to complement the talents of his core guys. And on the part of his young role players, he always knew how to get the best out of them. But it was never solely about the players' skills and capabilities. It all boiled down to their character and how they saw themselves as fitting pieces in the Spurs' system.

Pop described these ideal players as those that have "gotten over themselves." What he means is that he wanted players that look at the bigger picture instead of their accomplishments and numbers. For years, this has been the trend in what has become a two-decade San Antonio Spurs dynasty. It was a team that had zero problems with ego and one that had players who had fun playing with each other.

One can trace the roots of Gregg Popovich's ideal players all the way back to the time when David Robinson joined the team in 1989 when Pop was a mere assistant to Larry Brown. The Admiral was a humble MVP who did not mind handing the keys down to a young rookie Tim Duncan in 1997 when Gregg Popovich was in his second year as the team's head coach.

From then on, not only did Tim Duncan become the centerpiece of the entire franchise, but he also became the model athlete that embodied what Gregg Popovich wanted from his players. Timmy was simple, soft-spoken, and humble. He had no groupies, nor did he enjoy partying the nights away. He dressed like he shopped at a local thrift store. However, underneath the surface was a lion's heart beating and ready to compete and work hard every night. Duncan understood his role as the leader and best player but always played within the system that his coach wanted to run.

Character was what Gregg Popovich initially looked at whenever he scouted and traded for players. He looked for veterans that had experienced both losing and winning in the league. He valued those veterans' experience and how they had grown and matured in character more than how many years they had played in the league. Not only did the veterans bring in the experience of years of battling in the NBA but they also served as mentors for the younger guys.

When it came down to young guys, Pop even gave the overlooked guys a shot at a roster spot. For Pop, talent came second to character and IQ. That was why he valued Avery Johnson as his starting point guard when he was a young head coach, though the little man had been previously cut from the Spurs. Matt Bonner did not have any particular talent other than the fact that he could shoot the three-pointer well. The same was true for Danny Green. Gregg Popovich gave those players plenty of minutes when other teams would not have played them more than 20 games in a single season.

Gregg Popovich also valued how a player handled information. In the NBA, the blame game between coaches, players, and even management often gets played. When things did not go well, the blame got passed from one person to another. For Pop's part, he wanted his players to be accountable instead of shifting the blame. That was why it was important for him to have his players understand the value of handling information and criticism professionally.

Lastly, it was always important for Gregg Popovich to have players that were comfortable, not only with the guys they were playing with, but also with themselves. They had to know their strengths and roles to fit themselves into a diverse roster that had plenty of talent and skill. That was why Pop wanted his players to develop a sense of humor in order to let them feel comfortable with the entire organization.

Looking at the San Antonio Spurs 20 years after Gregg Popovich took over as the head coach, the team had become a group of guys that look like they are having fun on the floor no matter who is making the plays or shots. The players look comfortable passing to other players that would have otherwise not made it to a roster had they been drafted by another team. This was all due in large part to how Popovich looks for character above talent and how he instills the value of selflessness in a team that passes the ball around like no other.

The Stern Disciplinarian

Gregg Popovich always attacked a problem head-on and straightforward instead of circling matters that do not address the issue. The way he brings himself up in front of the media speaks volumes about his character. Pop answers questions with one-liners that make more sense than an entire essay other coaches would write to address any queries that the media might ask. Gregg Popovich was never afraid to speak his mind (albeit in short sentences) or do what he wanted to do. He was the same man in front of his players.

Having been trained at the Air Force Academy, Popovich became a strict disciplinarian. He knew the value of hard work and discipline, considering that he was once an impatient young man who wanted things to go his way in an instant. He learned the importance of discipline when he was with the Academy and he took those lessons to heart decades after leaving his old stomping grounds.

Popovich remained the same disciplinarian to his team. Pop often screamed and yelled at his players during live games and behind closed doors following team practices. He made it known not only to his players but also to the rest of the world how he felt. He forced his players into plays and positions on live television by continually screaming at them during games. And he did that to everyone on his team.

As prized of a friend and player that Tim Duncan had always been to Popovich, one of the greatest big men in league history was never spared from his coach's yells and criticisms either. Even Tony Parker, the man leading the point for the Spurs since 2001, got as much criticism from Pop as any other player. Gregg Popovich did not discriminate. He did not play favorites and always saw his players as single pieces of a larger puzzle. But despite all the criticisms and the yelling, he stayed beloved. Tony Parker would even say that the way Pop disciplined them was always tough but he knew it was the right thing to do at the end of the day because whatever Pop did was for the betterment of the team.[x]

The way Gregg Popovich disciplined everyone on the team equally has gotten the best out of everyone. Tony Parker might not have lived up to the expectations that Pop had of him when he gave him the starting spot and keys to the offense back in 2001 had he not worked harder because of Pop's way of pushing his players.

The same could be said about Manu Ginóbili, who surprised everyone by becoming an All-Star even after being chosen second-to-last back in the 1999 NBA Draft.

Even the role players maximized their talents because of how hard they were getting pushed. Over the past few seasons, Pop had taken players from different teams and made those organizations regret having given up on those guys. Boris Diaw was once waived by Charlotte but was an integral part of the 2014 Finals because of his ability to make crisp passes as a big man. Patty Mills, who played sparingly back in Portland, lost weight and became the backup point guard to Tony Parker. Danny Green was never wanted in Cleveland but he turned himself into the starting shooting guard of the San Antonio Spurs.

The way Popovich disciplined all of his players equally got the best out of his boys because they grew to understand that it was all for the sake of the team. In line with that equal treatment, Pop has given his players equal opportunities to show their strengths on the floor. The man at the end of the Spurs' bench even got more minutes than any other team's ninth man. This kind of a father-son disciplinarian relationship he had with the team was one of the things that made everyone better.

Popovich has also stated that this kind of fair treatment was what made other players want to play for the San Antonio Spurs.[xi] For instance, the 15-time All-Star and two-time MVP Tim Duncan had often been on the receiving end of insults and criticisms from Pop whenever he saw that his franchise player was not at his best. But conversely, whenever Timmy did something spectacular, Pop would give credit where it was due. It was a give-and-take relationship, not only with Tim Duncan but also with the entire roster.

Pop said that when everyone can see you get up in the face of one of the best players to have ever walked this planet, everyone would want to play for you. Popovich has always been a brutally honest man but he was also never afraid to give compliments whenever he saw a reason to. Of course, he never offered criticism when there were no reasons to do so, either. At the same time, this was why it was important for Pop to have players that could handle information and criticism well.

The Adaptability

The best coaches in the NBA typically stick to their systems without changing it once they found a lot of success running it. Take for instance the 11-time NBA champion Phil Jackson, who used the Triangle Offense to lead Michael Jordan to two separate three-peats. He also used the same system with different personnel and still found success when Shaquille O'Neal, Kobe Bryant, and Pau Gasol were the anchors.

Back in the 80s, Lakers head coach and now Miami Heat president Pat Riley used a variety of the run-and-gun systems affectionately called "Showtime," wherein he harnessed the passing skills of Magic Johnson to win four NBA titles. Years later, then-Phoenix Suns head coach Mike D'Antoni would implement a similar running style with his team but stressed spacing above anything else when it came down to playing the pick-and-roll.

A precise and established system has always been a winning NBA coach's identity. The Triangle was Jackson's calling card. Running and gunning were what made Riley and D'Antoni successful during their best years as head coaches. But when it comes to Gregg Popovich, whose success as an NBA coach can only be challenged by a handful of men, nobody could really say that he had an established system with the San Antonio Spurs.

All of the successful NBA coaches have had their players adapt to the system they want to run with the team. Jordan, who was so used to having the ball in his hands 90% of the time, had to move it around to adjust to Jackson's Triangle Offense. The same could be said about Bryant. But Pop has always been different. Instead of having his players adapt to his ideal system, he allows himself to adjust to his personnel and the talents they bring to the floor.[xii]

This is where player recruitment comes in. Gregg Popovich has always stressed character above talent and skill. That has been the reason why he goes out there to recruit and sign players that have a high basketball IQ that would be willing to adapt to change and handle any adversity that came their way. Those players must have the humility to understand their job with the team and step up to take bigger roles if needed.

Over the past decade, Gregg Popovich has had a knack for bringing in players that have become veterans in international competition. In 2014 when he won the title, he had foreign role players such as Marco Belinelli, Boris Diaw, Tiago Splitter, Patty Mills, and

Nando de Colo, among others. His love for international players stems from the fact that those men grew up and developed without the flash and ego that their more athletic American counterparts did. They make up for their lack of athleticism by focusing on the fundamentals and their basketball IQ. Such players have become perfect for Pop's ever-adjusting system.

Gregg Popovich's adaptability as a head coach demands that his players are just as diverse and willing to adjust. Since 1996, it has unquestionably worked to turn the San Antonio Spurs into the most consistent franchise over the last two decades. Pop has won championships by running different systems with the same core guys that were complemented by various role players.

For instance, back when he had David Robinson, he had the Admiral play a defense-oriented system to funnel opposing guards into the paint where the pair of seven-footers would intimidate them. He had his team play slowly during the early parts of the new millennium to adjust to his aging roster and the talents of Tim Duncan, who was never known as a fast player.

Back when Timmy was the center of the system, everything had to go through Duncan, though Pop would still stress the importance of ball movement. Attacking the paint was his focus, and he barely ever let his team shoot three-pointers. The slow pace worked to his advantage against teams that favored running the floor and speeding up the tempo. Pop would win four titles with that system.

But as the league transitioned into a faster pace, Gregg Popovich would evolve his offense into one that stressed speeding the tempo up and shooting more three-pointers. He had the same core trio of Duncan, Parker, and Ginóbili. But instead of having Timmy anchor the offense, he allowed Tony Parker to run the system freely. Along with younger core players that stretched the floor and shot three-pointers, Tony Parker's ability to get to the paint was crucial in making the San Antonio Spurs a successful pace-and-space team.

The way Gregg Popovich turned a slow and boring San Antonio Spurs into a team that ran the length of the court and stretched the floor while whipping the ball from corner to corner out on the perimeter was the inspiration to how present-day teams value ball movement and the three-point shot. Gregg Popovich masterfully adjusted a dead post-up system that ran through Duncan, to one where Tony Parker used screens to get to the basket and move the ball around, and now to one where defense and ball movement have been harmonized. This is a testament to the genius level of coaching that the man has.

While Gregg Popovich has always been lauded for his genius level of intellect in basketball, the five-time championship head coach has always viewed the game on a simplistic and objective level, to the point that he would even often call it boring.[x] True enough, it was very simple for him. He stuck to fundamentals despite several experts saying that it would take more than mere post-up plays or simple ball movement and jump shots to win titles. Just ask the 2003 San Antonio Spurs. Or, in another case, look at how the 2014 Spurs made three Miami Heat superstars look helpless.

The "simple" principle of Gregg Popovich's way of coaching was never about sticking to a certain system. He did not let his players run the Triangle 99% of the time, much like Phil Jackson did. He was not Mike D'Antoni in the sense that he forced his guys to run in every single play no matter what their ages were. What Pop did was maximize whatever skills and talents his players could offer, and routinely adjusted and promptly allowed changes to be implemented from time to time depending on the situation they were in.[x]

The legendary martial artist Bruce Lee once famously said:

"You must be shapeless, formless, like water. When you pour water in a cup, it becomes the cup. When you pour water in a bottle, it becomes the bottle. When you pour water in a teapot, it becomes the teapot. Water can drip, and it can crash. Become like water, my friend."

The same quote applies to how Gregg Popovich sees and approaches the role of coaching the San Antonio Spurs. He does not let his players adjust to what he wants to do or whatever system he wants to run. Pop is the water that takes the form of whatever personnel he has. He is a coach without an exact system. He is shapeless and formless. But the man has timelessly led his teams to championships and dominant regular season performances. Much like water, Pop has become the embodiment of what it is to adjust to the times of an ever-evolving NBA game and the diverse abilities of his players.

However, as time passes and age has caught up to Gregg Popovich, the NBA game has evolved to a point where teams are now shooting three-pointers like layups. The majority of the NBA has made it a point to focus more on the three-pointer as teams have learned the value of the shot and how inefficient post-up plays and midrange jumpers have become.

Gregg Popovich, who always hated the three-pointer regardless of how he utilized that shot to win a title in 2014, focused more on the traditional and fundamental style of basketball throughout the years after the Kawhi Leonard era. While the Spurs were still indeed successful, as they were able to get to the playoffs in all of those years except for the 2019-20 season, the new style of the NBA has seemingly become a bit of a challenge to Popovich. To remain relevant and successful in the modern NBA, it appears that he may once again have to change with the times.

Will he stay true to his beliefs in thinking that the three-point shot is just a gimmick? Will he stick to the fundamental plays of basketball instead of trying to embrace the three-pointer? Or will he adapt in a way that he still is able to hold onto his beliefs while leading a team to a possible championship run? Those are the new challenges that the legendary head coach needs to address in the future. After giving the world more than 20 years of excellence in the NBA, it will be interesting to see what Pop has in store for us next.

Chapter 5: How Gregg Popovich Maximizes Player Talent

The Fundamentals

Being the premier basketball league in the world, the level of skill and talent in the NBA is unmatched. Coaches have had the luxury of utilizing the most athletic and skillful players in the world while employing tactics and strategies fit only for exceptional talent. But Pop was never one to make the game of basketball complicated. One of the most basic principles that Gregg Popovich has lived by as a coach for the San Antonio Spurs has always been sticking to the fundamentals of basketball.

Save for the cat-quick Tony Parker and the freakishly gifted Kawhi Leonard, Pop has never had the luxury of being able to field some of those most athletic players the league has to offer. But for two decades, he has won titles and molded the Spurs into a model franchise by sticking to the fundamental skills needed from a basketball player.

Some of Pop's rotational players do not exactly excel in several aspects of the game. Some of them focus on playing a role exceptionally well to complement the core trio that Gregg Popovich has relied on so much. Bruce Bowen spent years on the Spurs roster defending the best perimeter players without having to so much as call his number for shots. Robert Horry won titles in San Antonio by stretching the floor and playing physical defense against opposing big men. Danny Green has gone from being unwanted in Cleveland to a starter in San Antonio, precisely because he sticks to playing defense and shooting jumpers from the outside.

No single player was expected to do everything for the team. Pop had Tim Duncan for post-up plays, inside scoring, and paint defense. He had Tony Parker making plays and breaking down the defense at the perimeter. Manu Ginóbili was there to give the team a lift off the bench. Kawhi Leonard shut down the opposing team's best players while also giving the team a lot of scoring over at the other end. Pop never expected any of his players to do everything at a high level. He wanted them to stick to their roles and to know the fundamentals by heart.

It has always been the fundamentals that make Pop's teams so competitive. Everyone has a role in the team. They stick to it. They own it. Despite how his players are often compacted into a singular role in the team, Gregg Popovich has always expected his players to know the fundamentals of basketball by heart. He wants guys that can shoot, defend, pass the ball, and know when to commit. These are not your prototypical jack-of-all-trades, so to speak, but Pop always expects them to embrace the fundamentals of basketball.

Popovich also teaches his players never to skip a process. He always trains them to start out from the basics of passing, catching, shooting, rebounding, and defense before he goes on to the more challenging concepts. One assistant coach would describe the Spurs as a junior varsity team. But the message he always relayed through those sessions was that the fundamentals would always be more important than any other skill in basketball. If all else fails, you will always have your basics to bail you out of a funk.[xi]

This is the exact reason why every incarnation of Gregg Popovich's San Antonio Spurs has stuck to the fundamentals. Back in the grind-it-out slow-paced era, Pop had his players throw the ball to Timmy down at the low post and would play off his ability to score inside the paint or make plays for others. In the pace-and-space era, he had Parker breaking down defenses with the pick-and-roll. The ball movement and outside sniping comes after defenders struggle to commit and rotate back on defense. Those were simplistic systems that Pop ran in San Antonio, yet it won titles because his players mastered the plays and embraced playing the fundamental aspect of the game.

Equal Opportunity

While Gregg Popovich has time and time again relied heavily on Duncan, Parker, and Ginóbili, the rest of the 15-man roster has arguably been more important to him than his Big Three. Pop allowed everyone on his team to play no matter how young or old they were. Back in the 2000s, he had a knack for picking up old veterans for their experience. Even those beyond age 35 found a home in San Antonio because of how Pop uses their expertise and veteran instincts to his advantage.

But the biggest development that Pop has made in the NBA as far as role players are concerned is how he has allowed his younger players to grow. Gregg Popovich is a man of equal opportunity. Back in 2014, nobody on the team played more than 30 minutes a game and yet they won the title. He gave more than 20 minutes a night to Patty Mills, whom the Portland Trail Blazers had drafted but used sparingly. Danny Green barely saw time in Cleveland before he became the starting shooting guard for the San Antonio Spurs. Marco Belinelli went from playing 10 to 15 minutes a night elsewhere to shooting 43% from the three-point area while playing 25 minutes in San Antonio. Jonathon Simmons bounced from league to league before the Spurs gave him a chance in 2015. Now he plays good minutes as a backup wing. Even Dewayne Dedmon, who had three teams in the 2013-14 season alone, started a few games in place of Pau Gasol for the Spurs during the 2016-17 season.

The way Gregg Popovich gave his players equal opportunities often became a point of criticism. In certain stretches of the season, Pop would rest his Big Three and several of his starters to allow his role players to run the team on their own. He would even do it against the toughest opponents and in nationally-televised games to the dismay of NBA executives.

But for all the nights off that Gregg Popovich allowed his core players to have, the bench never failed to impress the league. Pop continued winning games though he ran the offense through backup players because of the confidence he instilled in everyone on the team. While the long-term goal of resting starters was often seen as a tactic to preserve legs in preparation for the playoffs, Pop did it to not only freshen up his core players but also to allow his role guys a chance to increase their confidence level. There was never a player on Pop's bench that was not ready to step onto the court and do his part at any given moment.

Some may say that Gregg Popovich had been doing that just to troll his opponents. He once did it when the Spurs faced the Miami Heat during the 2013-14 season in a rematch of the 2013 NBA Finals. Pop rested all his starters in a nationally-televised game but almost came out with the win, even though he played with bench guys. He might even have been playing possum just to keep other teams from gauging the Spurs' real potential. No one knows for certain what goes on in his mind. But the only thing one can be sure of is that Pop spreads the minutes out and allows everyone on the team to play.

If America is the land of equal opportunity, then Gregg Popovich has embraced that mantra and made the San Antonio Spurs a place for older players to re-invent themselves or for the younger ones to develop their skills. Pop has made it a point to shuffle his minutes and give a chance to players that would have otherwise been cut in other teams or might not have even been signed to an NBA contract.

Love for Food and Dining

As a man who is widely known for being one of the greatest strategists in basketball history and as a coach who has been one of the best leaders when it comes to making the most out of what his players could give, it might seem odd to think that Gregg Popovich's love for food and dining has somehow also made an impact in how he was able to make his team and players better over the years.

To say the least, Gregg Popovich's identity as a food enthusiast and wine connoisseur has a close and direct relationship to how he has been able to become the model leader in an organization and how he has been able to maximize the talents that his players have. As odd as it might sound, this is a part of Popovich that has always been widely talked about in NBA coaching circles and by his former players because of how it allowed them to play better as a team.

The story of Gregg Popovich's love of food and wine can be traced all the way back to when he was in the Air Force. Pop, when he was stationed in Northern California in a town just two hours away from Napa, frequently visited wineries during his spare time. While Napa back then was yet to become one of the world's most popular wine destinations, Popovich learned the value of great wine and had studied the art and industry ever since. Visiting popular restaurants and wineries with the best selection of wines eventually became a hobby for him.[xiii]

When Gregg Popovich landed his first gig as a head coach with Pomona-Pitzer, he made it a point to have his team bond over dinner and good wine, regardless of how lean the budget was or how modest his salary was back then. No matter what the costs were, he always found a way to make sure that his players had good food waiting for them on a near-daily basis when he was still coaching that Division III school. Tim Dignan, a player who played under Popovich at Pomona-Pitzer back in the day, said that the head coach always made sure that they were fed well. In some instances, they would even travel to popular destinations just so they could experience what it was like to eat there. The key for Popovich at that time was to see to it that his players and coaching staff had at least one memorable meal together as a team. And when the budget was slim, something as simple as eating in Gregg Popovich's apartment was already a memorable way for them to bond.[xiii]

Make no mistake about it. The X's and O's were always important in basketball and your players' individual strengths and weaknesses were also just as important when it came to maximizing what they had to offer. However, something as simple as sharing a meal together with everyone on the team was always one of the ways that Popovich was able to get his entire team in one place so that they could all learn more about one another in the process of bonding.

With Pop putting so much emphasis on team dining, it became a habit and a tradition for him, to the point that he once said his ultimate legacy as a head coach was "food and wine" when he was asked by a reporter on the legacy he would leave to the NBA when all was said and done. In some ways, he was joking. But in other ways, he was telling the truth.

There has always been something valuable in Gregg Popovich's approach as a food and wine enthusiast, especially when it came down to treating his players the right way whenever they would go out and dine. One case in point was in 2010 when the San Antonio Spurs suffered a loss to the Dallas Mavericks in a pivotal Game 5 of their playoff series. Popovich did not let his staff and players linger on the loss. Instead, he had his staff convene in his hotel suite and told them to make reservations with a good restaurant and have everyone on the team eat there. In that sense, he allowed his players to feel like they were still special to him by treating them right, and by making them feel less bad about that loss they had just suffered. Pop ultimately told them that night that losing was a part of basketball but going right back to work the next day after a loss was the more important aspect they should be focusing on.

The words that Gregg Popovich spoke to his players that night could have been relayed through a simple text message or during a team meeting in practice. He could have even just asked his staff to relay that message to his players. However, the simple act of asking them out to a good dinner in a reputable restaurant with some of the best food the locality had to offer made them think and realize that, even at the worst of times, they were still a team and that their coach still had their backs.

One of the more telling situations where Gregg Popovich never forgot about the value of making his team feel like family through something as simple as dining out was when he made reservations to a good restaurant in Miami prior to their Game 6 matchup with the Heat during the 2013 NBA Finals. That reservation was hopefully to be for celebratory purposes in case they would win the championship that night. But, as we all know, Ray Allen's series-saving three-pointer happened and the Spurs went home that night with their heads hung.

Instead of canceling the reservations and allowing his players to regroup on their own following the heartbreaking loss, Gregg Popovich preached the value of family by telling them to go straight to the restaurant. He made it a point to talk to everyone on the team during the dinner to make it easier for them to swallow that bad loss in Game 6. That way, he was able to highlight his leadership skills and maximize what his players had to offer as he basically tried to resuscitate them back to life with something as simple as family dinner together.

As Danny Green, a prominent role player who won a championship with the San Antonio Spurs under Gregg Popovich, said, team dinners for them were one of the ways they could connect with one another and try to learn more about each other's strengths and weaknesses so that they could eventually discover ways of maximizing each other's potential on the floor when it was time for them to suit up and play together. Even Pau Gasol, who had played under Phil Jackson in two championship runs with the Lakers, said that he had never been part of an organization with a culture that is as close to what Gregg Popovich established with his habit of taking his team out for dinner and wine. Gasol said that players knew the importance of something that simple and how important it was for Pop to be able to host those team dinners.[xiii]

In one case, an unnamed former Spurs player said that being with the San Antonio Spurs organization under Gregg Popovich allowed him to be friends with every single player on the roster for the first time in his career. While players practice, train, and play with their teammates for years, it is quite normal for them to treat each other only professionally, in the sense that they are not friends outside the court. But, in Pop's case, the fact that he was able to have his team eat dinners together frequently allowed his players to become friends with one another. There is always something special about knowing your teammates more outside of the court.

If you are able to make friends and deeply connect with a person you work with, regardless of whether you are athletes or are in the corporate world, it makes things easier for you to work well with one another and maximize each other's productivity because you have formed a bond that reaches well beyond the realms of professionalism. It is like when you understand family members and close friends better in any kind of situation without even having them utter a single word. The fact that you are able to learn things about one another and share a lasting bond together gives you a level of familiarity that cannot be achieved with five-hour practices in the gym or with video sessions during team meetings.

Another point to take into consideration was the fact that table reservations are made in large groups because Gregg Popovich did not want his players to split into groups or certain friendship cliques. He wanted all of his players to get to know each other, star players and bench players alike.

In Popovich's case, hosting team dinners was not only a way for him to keep his players' morale and chemistry up while also allowing his players to get to know one another. It was also a way for him to get to know his players' personal lives better and for him to understand how they think. That way, it was easier for him to assess how to maximize his players' strengths and determine how to make the most out of what a certain guy had to offer the team in certain situations on the court.

Because of how long Gregg Popovich had been hosting team dinners in fancy Michelin Star restaurants, the practice has become more than just a habit for the San Antonio Spurs, it has become an ingrained part of their culture. And the best thing about it was that Pop would always pick up the tab.

Even something that is well outside the realm of basketball can have a huge impact on how your team plays and how your players interact with one another on the court. That is why, in corporate situations, it has always been a practice for the best leaders to arrange bonding activities with the people they are working with so that they will be able to get to know one another on a deeper level. Doing something this simple might not mean a lot to those who value the numbers alone. But something as intangible as bonding over dinner with your team fosters a good working relationship that cannot be replaced by hundreds of hours working in the office or on the court together.

These bonding experiences were a unique aspect of Pop's mentorship that gave his team a deep sense of friendship and belonging that always strengthened their regard and their commitment to each other and to the Spurs as a whole.

Chapter 6: Gregg Popovich, the Leader

Strong leadership is what has made great nations into what they are today. The ability to make others follow without question and the undying dedication to achieve success makes one a great leader no matter what standard you look at. The greatest presidents, generals, and even insurgents have had an impact on society precisely because of how they led their people towards their cause.

In basketball, it has been Gregg Popovich's sense of leadership that has created an unprecedented culture of winning in San Antonio. Coupled with the system he has put in place in the Spurs franchise, Pop's leadership has made a small market team and otherwise unsuccessful organization into the model of consistency and greatness that it is today.

The way he chooses his personnel, players, and coaching staff speaks volumes about how he leads through preparation. Egos are thrown out the window.

It was never about "I" in San Antonio. It was all about the team and their goals of becoming great every single season. That was what led Gregg Popovich to choose who he wanted to be on the roster and who he wanted to spend time with as a coach.

His strong personality and fearless nature as a mentor and disciplinarian were what drove his players to excel and work harder. Gregg Popovich was never afraid to speak his mind. Don Nelson knew this when Pop was with the Warriors as an assistant. That was why he acted as a liaison between Nelly and Chris Webber. He stayed the same when he started coaching the Spurs.

In San Antonio, he chastised everyone who failed to bring in the results he desired. He did that with David Robinson, Tim Duncan, Tony Parker, and Kawhi Leonard. Pop got his players to work hard by motivating them with both praise and criticism. He managed egos almost to perfection while allowing players to grow in confidence. He gave roles with definiteness and made sure his players knew for a fact that they were small integral pieces of a larger success.

As a coach leading a group of assistants, Gregg Popovich was never controlling, nor was he a man who tried to dictate what others should think. He learned that when he was working under Larry Brown. Brown encouraged Pop to give comments and make suggestions that were unorthodox and new. Pop went on to do the same with his assistants in San Antonio.

Ettore Messina, a celebrated head coach in the EuroLeague, gave up his status as the best coach in Europe to become an assistant under Pop in San Antonio. This is a prime example of how desirable it was to work with Popovich. Everyone within the industry wanted to be exposed to the brilliance of the five-time champion head coach. Messina described Gregg Popovich as being like an ancient Greek philosopher that spent time encouraging discussions among fellow men to find the truth. Pop did the same as a head coach.

Messina would say that Gregg Popovich pushed his assistants to argue with him and amongst each other to promote a healthy discourse of ideas that would make the team better. Despite that, he never forgot to treat everyone like family and to make everyone else on the team think the same way. Messina said that Popovich cared about everyone in the organization and what they thought. The Spurs were a family first before it became a basketball team for Pop.[xiv]

With Gregg Popovich's ability to lead by example and to genuinely care about his players as well as his staff as a disciplined mentor, he has earned the respect of the entire league. Coaches look up to him. Even players that have never had a chance to play for him treat him with respect and adoration for what he has done for the Spurs organization.

When he was once asked about who he looked up to, Gregg Popovich did not have much to say. He has always tried to avoid idolizing and looking up to people other than the ones he knows personally and those who have played an integral part in his life. He rarely notes any admiration for the famous leaders in history. He would rather choose to admire those close to him because he knows those people.[xv]

It is his ability to lead as a humble man with a simple upbringing that has made Gregg Popovich one of the most adored figures in league history. Even the media, which he has a knack for trolling, loves him for whatever tiny bits of information he gives them. Everyone who has had the pleasure of working under him always had only the best things to say about the way he led the team. Pop is a genuine leader both on and off the court.

Chapter 7: Key Takeaways

Character

The most important aspect of Gregg Popovich's coaching was finding players that fit his idea of someone who had the perfect character for the Spurs' system. Pop wanted players that were willing to sacrifice personal ideals and desires to buy into a team setup. He valued character above any other aspect of a basketball player. He did not even particularly care about a player's talent as long as they were good enough to get to the NBA. What mattered more to Popovich was a player's attitude.

Rarely do you see Gregg Popovich and the San Antonio Spurs trade for or sign players who exhibit selfish or individualistic behavior. It has always been a roster of players that are willing to sacrifice minutes, stats, and individual awards and glory for the sake of making the Spurs consistent winners and championship contenders. This has been going on for two decades already. While championship teams have come and gone, the Spurs remained consistent because of how they looked for players that had the proper character and attitude needed for their unselfish system. This is also why you have rarely seen much personal drama involving the Spurs. They are a team with a similar mindset that works together in harmony under Pop's steady leadership.

Relying on the Fundamentals

Another key aspect of Gregg Popovich's system has been his reliance on the fundamental skills of basketball, such as shooting, rebounding, passing, and proper defense. Rarely did the Spurs have flashy highlight-reel types of players because Pop preferred those that had already mastered the fundamental skills. His system has been all about fundamentals, from the slow-paced era of Robinson and Duncan to the pace-and-space style of the 2014 championship team.

What Gregg Popovich did was take the simple fundamentals of basketball and got his players to master them to a level that no other team in the NBA could match. Looking back at the early days of his coaching career, no other team in the league could grind it out and score from the post like the Spurs did because Pop instilled the habit of mastering the basics of playing a slow-paced defensive style. And when the Spurs dominated the league with their offense in their pace-and-space era, no other team moved the ball or their players as well as the Spurs did. While they were not necessarily the best three-point shooters or inside scorers, their ability to find open teammates by moving the ball and going around the court created open opportunities from all areas of the floor. It sounds so simple, but Gregg Popovich has been able to win by relying on those fundamentals.

Adapting to Change

Nothing in this world ever stays exactly the same. As the famous saying goes, "The only thing that is constant is change." Everything is bound to change and evolve someday. Humans evolve. Animals evolve. The world around us is ever-changing. And of course, change also occurs in sports such as basketball. The NBA game itself has undergone numerous changes since its early days in the 1940s.

Everything about the NBA changes. The rules, players, and styles all change. Teams have changed. Even the standard of winning basketball has changed. But since taking over the team in 1996, Gregg Popovich has always adjusted to whatever changes the NBA has undergone. He has adapted to different eras and styles in his two decades of coaching and still found ways to win.

Gregg Popovich never strictly adhered to one style. His teams' style changed depending on the era and the competition they faced year by year. When Duncan and Robinson roamed the paint, he relied on a slow-paced style that focused on inside scoring. When Parker and his younger players matured, he had the Spurs running and gunning from the outside as an answer to the league's reliance on guards and the three-point shot. And when Kawhi Leonard took over the reins of the Spurs, Pop used the versatility of his gifted two-way superstar to make San Antonio an adaptive two-way team that played both ends of the floor equally well.

The importance of studying and learning from how Popovich adapted to the change of his personnel and the growing demands of the NBA can never be understated. What his long-term success demonstrates is that there truly is no single formula for winning. Pop knew that and changed the way his team played to adapt to whatever was needed from them to win titles or at least contend for one. One should never be so stubborn as to refuse to accept change and adapt to it.

Take it from Pop, who never failed to adjust to the ever-changing norms of basketball.

Chapter 8: Conclusion and Legacy

One would immediately point out that the single greatest legacy of Gregg Popovich in the world of basketball was how he built the entire San Antonio Spurs organization into the model franchise that it has been for the last 20 years. Nobody would argue with that. It has always been a truth that never ceases to amaze everyone that has closely followed basketball over the past two decades.

Five championships over a span of 20 seasons is not exactly an unprecedented accomplishment. The Lakers won the same amount of titles in the same time span. The Celtics had 11 back in the early days of the NBA. The Chicago Bulls won six championships in a span of only eight seasons. On paper, Gregg Popovich's five championships in more than 20 years do not seem like a one-of-a-kind achievement.

However, what screams "dynasty" is not the number of titles that Pop actually won in the two decades he has coached the Spurs. It is the consistency and the ever-evolving way he has coached his team to become contenders year in and year out that has made him one of the best coaches and leaders the league has ever seen. Since 1998, San Antonio never fell under 50 wins in a full regular season. Those 20 seasons include 6 years of leading the Spurs to at least 60 wins during the regular season. It has been a pattern of consistency for Gregg Popovich to make sure that his Spurs are one of the title favorites every season, even when former contenders came and went. There was never any such thing as a "rebuilding season" for Pop. Pop was *always* building and strengthening his team—and dominating at the same time.

There have been one-hit wonders in the league and dynasties that lasted for about five seasons before dropping into obscurity for several more seasons. But Gregg Popovich consistently coached the San Antonio

Spurs to strong playoff appearances and several seasons of fighting against contenders that have come and gone. The Laker dynasty in the early 2000s has long been gone. The Celtic dynasty lasted a few seasons after winning a title in 2008. The Miami Heat won two titles before breaking it up after five years of partnership. While other teams came and went, the San Antonio Spurs stayed on top of the food chain while keeping the same core players that catapulted the team to greatness for the past two decades.

What makes a good leader is also the impact they have left behind in the lives of their former pupils. The Greek philosopher Aristotle was a student of Plato. Plato, in turn, was a student of Socrates. Great leaders and great minds shape the younger generations into becoming just as impactful. This was also a mark and legacy that Gregg Popovich will ultimately leave behind in the NBA.

Just as Gregg Popovich was once a student of the great Larry Brown, he molded and mentored more than a handful of future leaders that have all found their respective niches in the NBA as successful coaches. One of Pop's first assistants to become a head coach was Mike Brown, who started leading the Cleveland Cavaliers in 2005. While Brown had the indomitable LeBron James, it was not easy to lead the Cavs to two consecutive seasons as the best team during the regular season on the strength of one player alone.

After Mike Brown, there was also Mike Budenholzer, who worked under Pop as an assistant since 1996. He started coaching the Atlanta Hawks in 2013 and has since led them to a season wherein they won 60 games and clinched the top seed in the Eastern Conference. The way Atlanta plays an unselfish style of basketball predicated on ball movement is closely reminiscent of how Pop coached the Spurs. Hawks assistant coaches Taylor Jenkins and Ben Sullivan also worked under Pop a few seasons back.

Several members of the coaching staff and front office of the Brooklyn Nets are also players and coaches that have worked under Gregg Popovich in the past. These include Nets General Manager Sean Marks, who played for San Antonio back in the early to middle 2000s. Marks' assistant, Trajan Langdon, also worked as a scout for the Spurs a few seasons back. Jacque Vaughn, an assistant coach for the Nets, once played for the Spurs and was also an assistant in San Antonio.

In Dallas, the Mavericks were once coached by Avery Johnson, who was Gregg Popovich's beloved starting point guard back when he first started coaching the Spurs. Johnson would lead the Mavericks past the Spurs in 2006 to make an appearance in the NBA Finals. Now, former Spurs player Michael Finley works as the assistant vice president of basketball operations for the Dallas Mavericks.

The celebrated rookie champion head coach Steve Kerr of the Golden State Warriors was a former Spurs player after moving on from the championship years in Chicago post-Michael Jordan. Kerr has brought the pace-and-space style to Golden State and made it even better to the point that the system looked as if it were on steroids thanks to the bevy of superstars and shooters that the Warriors field every night.

Alvin Gentry of the New Orleans Pelicans once served as an assistant to Gregg Popovich but has seen a successful stint with the Phoenix Suns in the late 2000s. He brought in the Spurs' brand of defense while playing the D'Antoni style of offense to bring the Suns within a few games away from making the Finals back in 2010. He also went on to coach the New Orleans Pelicans well enough despite their lack of depth and talent.

Given how we could go on and on with this list, what becomes evident is that Gregg Popovich is not only a master tactician and strategist, but he has also become the ideal teacher for hopeful minds. He has passed on knowledge not only to his assistants but also to his former players, who have all seen success as executives or as coaches themselves. The Popovich brand of leadership is one that encompasses the entire locker organization and one that transcends the Spurs franchise. It allows people to mold themselves into leaders. His influence continues to spread out and permeate the world of basketball in a way that will resonate for many generations to come.

As one looks to the future of Gregg Popovich himself, another title or two might or might not be on the horizon for the venerable, elder statesman of the league. At an advanced age of over 70, Pop may soon retire. In truth, he could have retired already—and he and contemplated doing just that a few years ago, but he instead chose to push himself further. And it was the right decision since he won a championship just a year after he contemplated hanging his coaching boots up. But as for the future? Well, the shot clock is winding down.

The man that was once regarded as a father figure is now a "grandfather" figure to many players and coaches that have had the pleasure of working with him. The lasting impact he has had in building the Spurs franchise and in developing future minds are legacies that will last for decades, long after he has departed from the organization.

As Sun Tzu once said in the *Art of War*:

"Military tactics are like unto water; for water in its natural course runs away from high places and hastens downwards. So in war, the way is to avoid what is strong and to strike at what is weak. Water shapes its course according to the nature of the ground over which it flows; the soldier works out his victory in relation to the foe whom he is facing. Therefore, just as water retains no constant shape, so in warfare there are no constant conditions. He who can modify his tactics in relation to his opponent and thereby succeed in winning, may be called a heaven-born captain."

In this sense, Gregg Popovich has long been the water that flowed through the NBA for two decades. He had no particular form but adjusted accordingly to what was needed from him. He built on the strength of his leadership adapted to face the conditions of an ever-evolving league. Just like a river, he has branched out, spreading his knowledge and wisdom, into smaller streams that would soon become rivers on their own. And just like water, Gregg Popovich's legacy will forever live on.

Final Word/About the Author

I was born and raised in Norwalk, Connecticut. Growing up, I could often be found spending many nights watching basketball, soccer, and football matches with my father in the family living room. I love sports and everything that sports can embody. I believe that sports are one of the most genuine forms of competition, heart, and determination. I write my works to learn more about influential athletes and coaches in the hopes that from my writing, you the reader can walk away inspired to put in an equal if not greater amount of hard work and perseverance to pursue your goals. If you enjoyed *Gregg Popovich: The Inspiring Life and Leadership Lessons of One of Basketball's Greatest Coaches,* please leave a review! Also, you can read more of my works on *David Ortiz, Mike Trout, Bryce Harper, Jackie Robinson, Aaron Judge, Odell Beckham Jr., Bill Belichick, Serena Williams, Rafael Nadal, Roger Federer, Novak Djokovic, Richard Sherman, Andrew Luck, Rob*

Gronkowski, Brett Favre, Calvin Johnson, Drew Brees, J.J. Watt, Colin Kaepernick, Aaron Rodgers, Peyton Manning, Tom Brady, Russell Wilson, Odell Beckham Jr., Bill Belichick, Charles Barkley, Trae Young, Gregg Popovich, Pat Riley, John Wooden, Steve Kerr, Brad Stevens, Red Auerbach, Doc Rivers, Erik Spoelstra, Michael Jordan, LeBron James, Kyrie Irving, Klay Thompson, Stephen Curry, Kevin Durant, Russell Westbrook, Anthony Davis, Chris Paul, Blake Griffin, Kobe Bryant, Joakim Noah, Scottie Pippen, Carmelo Anthony, Kevin Love, Grant Hill, Tracy McGrady, Vince Carter, Patrick Ewing, Karl Malone, Tony Parker, Allen Iverson, Hakeem Olajuwon, Reggie Miller, Michael Carter-Williams, John Wall, James Harden, Tim Duncan, Steve Nash, Draymond Green, Kawhi Leonard, Dwyane Wade, Ray Allen, Pau Gasol, Dirk Nowitzki, Jimmy Butler, Paul Pierce, Manu Ginobili, Pete Maravich, Larry Bird, Kyle Lowry, Jason Kidd, David Robinson, LaMarcus Aldridge, Derrick Rose, Paul George, Kevin Garnett, Chris

Paul, Marc Gasol, Yao Ming, Al Horford, Amar'e Stoudemire, DeMar DeRozan, Isaiah Thomas, Kemba Walker, Chris Bosh, Andre Drummond, JJ Redick, DeMarcus Cousins, Wilt Chamberlain, Bradley Beal, Rudy Gobert, Aaron Gordon, Kristaps Porzingis, Nikola Vucevic, Andre Iguodala, Devin Booker, John Stockton, Jeremy Lin, Chris Paul, Pascal Siakam, Jayson Tatum, Gordon Hayward, Nikola Jokic, Bill Russell, Victor Oladipo, Luka Doncic, Ben Simmons, Shaquille O'Neal, Joel Embiid, Donovan Mitchell, Damian Lillard and *Giannis Antetokounmpo* in the Kindle Store. If you love basketball, check out my website at claytongeoffreys.com to join my exclusive list where I let you know about my latest books and give you lots of goodies.

Like what you read? Please leave a review!

I write because I love sharing the stories of influential coaches like Gregg Popovich with fantastic readers like you. My readers inspire me to write more so please do not hesitate to let me know what you thought by leaving a review! If you love books on life, sports, or productivity, check out my website at claytongeoffreys.com to join my exclusive list where I let you know about my latest books. Aside from being the first to hear about my latest releases, you can also download a free copy of *33 Life Lessons: Success Principles, Career Advice & Habits of Successful People*. See you there!

Clayton

References

[i] Hamnik, Al. "NBA's Gregg Popovich Returning to His Region Roots". *NWI Times*. 11 October 2010. Web

[ii] MacMullan, Jackie. "Gregg Popovich will Lead the Team he was Left Off Four Decades Ago." *ESPN*. 23 August 2016. Web

[iii] Monroe, Mike. "Relationship Building, Hard Work Helped Popovich Rise From Humble Start". *Express News*. 20 October 2014. Web

[iv] Abrams, Jonathan. "Pop's First Rodeo". *Bleacher Report*. 14 November 2016. Web

[v] Young, Jabari. "Parker-Popovich Relationship Resembles What Spurs Coach Had With Duncan". *Express News*. 13 February 2017. Web

[vi] Hancox, Kyle. "Gregg Popovich and the San Antonio Spurs: 20 Years in the Making". *Give Me Sport*. 2015. Web

[vii] MacMullan, Jackie. "How Spurs' Majestic 2014 Finals Performance Changed the NBA". *ESPN*. 2015 June 2010. Web

[viii] Zucker, Joseph. "Gregg Popovich says Kawhi Leonard wasn't a leader with the Spurs". *Bleacher Report*. 25 November 2018. Web

[ix] Zucker, Joseph. "Gregg Popovich says he's hated three 3-point shot for 20 years". *Bleacher Report*. 30 November 2018. Web

[x] Allen, Jeff. "Gregg Popovich: In Pop We Trust". *Rolling Stones*. 2 June 2014. Web

[xi] Davis, Scott. "Gregg Popovich Has A Brilliant Philosophy On Handling Players, And It Exemplifies The Spurs' Unprecedented Run Of Success". *Business Insider*. 18 March 2016. Web

[xii] Baranko, Kyle. "San Antonio Spurs: The Secret Genius of Gregg Popovich". *Fan Sided*. 21 March 2016. Web

[xiii] Holmes, Baxter. "Michelin restaurants and fabulous wines: Inside the secret team dinners that have built the Spurs' dynasty". *ESPN*. 25 July 2020. Web

[xiv] Manfred, Tony. "55-Year-Old Legend Who Quit His Job To Work For The Spurs Explains Why Gregg Popovich Is A Genius". *Business Insider*. 5 December 2014. Web

[xv] Robinson, Brandon. "Strong Leadership Has Been Key to Gregg

Popovich's Success". *CBS Sports*. 17 May 2016. Web

Made in United States
North Haven, CT
07 March 2023